JESUS
SWEETEST NAME I KNOW

WHO JESUS IS
AND WHY IT MATTERS

by

pam gillaspie

Jesus: Sweetest Name I Know

Copyright © 2013 by Pam Gillaspie
Published by
Precept Ministries International
P.O. Box 182218
Chattanooga, Tennessee 37422
www.precept.org

ISBN 978-1-934884-78-2

Dedicated to . . .

My dear friend, Jordie. I wish God had made you a northerner for life, but I'm glad He crossed our paths for the time that He did!

Acknowledgements

I always feel a little embarrassed having my name on the cover of a book when I know the truth: every book is a group project. Rick Purdy and Pete DeLacy, you not only bring clarity to my writing, you teach me along the way. With every manuscript that passes through your hands I become a better thinker and writer because of your investment in me. Cress and Alison, thank you so much for your work in proofreading and reference checking. Mary Ann, thanks for keeping our classes running so I can focus on the writing. Staci, BJ, David, Ryan, Kristin, Scott, John, Brian, Kathleen, Paula, and Kellie: I'm humbled by the all of the work that you do getting the word out and putting the study in people's hands.

Special thanks to Kay for setting an example of handling God's Word accurately and consistently speaking the truth even when it's unpopular and to Jan Priddy and Jan Silvious for always encouraging me in the work God has called me to and believing in me even when I've doubted.

Thank you to my family—Mom and Dad, Dave, Brad, and Katie—there are neither adequate nor sufficient words to tell you my heart for each of you.

Finally and foremost, all glory to God—Father, Son, and Holy Spirit—the rest of us are simply servants.

JESUS

SWEETEST NAME I KNOW

WHO JESUS IS AND WHY IT MATTERS

There is nothing quite like your favorite pair of jeans. You can dress them up, you can dress them down. You can work in them, play in them, shop in them . . . live in them. They always feel right. It is my hope that the structure of this Bible study will fit you like those jeans; that it will work with your life right now, right where you are whether you're new to this whole Bible thing or whether you've been studying the Book for years!

How is this even possible? Smoke and mirrors, perhaps? The new mercilessly thrown in the deep end? The experienced given pompoms and the job of simply cheering others on? None of the above.

Sweeter than Chocolate!® flexible studies are designed with options that will allow you to go as deep each week as you desire. If you're just starting out and feeling a little overwhelmed, stick with the main text and don't think a second thought about the sidebar assignments. If you're looking for a challenge, then take the sidebar prompts and go ahead and dig all the way to China! As you move along through the study, think of the sidebars and "Digging Deeper" boxes as that 2% of lycra that you find in certain jeans . . . the wiggle-room that will help them fit just right.

Beginners may find that they want to start adding in some of the optional assignments as they go along. Experts may find that when three children are throwing up for three days straight, foregoing those assignments for the week is the way to live wisely.

Life has a way of ebbing and flowing and this study is designed to ebb and flow right along with it!

Enjoy!

JESUS
SWEETEST NAME I KNOW

WHO JESUS IS AND WHY IT MATTERS

An Inductive Study of Christology

How to use this study

Sweeter than Chocolate!® studies meet you where you are and take you as far as you want to go.

1. WEEKLY STUDY: The main text guides you through the complete topic of study for the week.

2. FYI boxes: For Your Information boxes provide bite-sized material to shed additional light on the topic.

> **FYI:**
>
> **Reading Tip: Begin with prayer**
> You may have heard this a million times over and if this is a million and one, so be it. Whenever you read or study God's Word, first pray and ask His Spirit to be your Guide.

3. ONE STEP FURTHER and other sidebar boxes: Sidebar boxes give you the option to push yourself a little further. If you have extra time or are looking for an extra challenge, you can try one, all, or any number in between! These boxes give you the ultimate in flexibility.

> **ONE STEP FURTHER:**
>
> **Word Study: *torah*/law**
> The first of eight Hebrew key words we encounter for God's Word is *torah* translated "law." If you're up for a challenge this week, do a word study to learn what you can about *torah*. Run a concordance search and examine where the word *torah* appears in the Old Testament and see what you can learn from the contexts.
>
> If you decide to look for the word for "law" in the New Testament, you'll find that the primary Greek word is *nomos*.
>
> Be sure to see what Paul says about the law in Galatians 3 and what Jesus says in Matthew 5.

4. DIGGING DEEPER boxes: If you're looking to go further, Digging Deeper sections will help you sharpen your skills as you continue to mine the truths of Scripture for yourself.

> **Digging Deeper**
>
> **What else does God's Word say about counselors?**
>
> If you can, spend some time this week digging around for what God's Word says about counselors.
>
> Start by considering what you already know about counsel from the Word of God and see if you can actually show where these truths are in the Bible. Make sure that the Word actually says what you think it says.

JESUS
SWEETEST NAME I KNOW

WHO JESUS IS AND WHY IT MATTERS

An Inductive Study of Christology

Week One
Who Do You Say I Am?

Jesus said to his disciples, "But who do you say that I am?"
–Matthew 16:15

It is the ultimate question and people answer it in a myriad of ways: *Who do you say Jesus is?*

During His time on earth, people knew Jesus was more than a carpenter. In fact many figured He was more than a man. Something about Him was different. Normal people don't walk on water. Typical guys don't raise the dead. Some, like Peter, knew who He was. Others pegged Him for a resurrected prophet, possibly John the Baptist, Elijah, or Jeremiah.

Who is He? was a huge question in the first century and it remains the ultimate question today. It is the primary question of this study because it is the primary question of life.

In the end it won't matter what your mom or your spouse or your pastor said about Jesus. The question is yours to answer: *Who do you say He is?*

FYI:

If You're in a Class
Complete **Week One** together on your first day of class. This will be a great way to start getting to know one another and will help those who are newer to Bible study get their bearings.

Week One: **Who Do You Say I Am?**

CONSIDER the WAY you THINK

As we start our study, we need to examine our presuppositions. Each of us will come to a better understanding of *why* we believe what we believe. For now, let's consider what views we're bringing to table.

How would you answer the question Jesus posed to Peter: *Who do you say I am?*

Why?

When did you come to this view?

What do you base your beliefs on?

What questions do you hope to find answers for during this study?

JESUS
SWEETEST NAME I KNOW

WHO JESUS IS AND WHY IT MATTERS

An Inductive Study of Christology

Digging Deeper

What do others think about Jesus?

How does the world view Jesus today? What false views do you encounter regularly? If you have some time this week, find out some false beliefs about Jesus. False religions and philosophies always stray from biblical views of Jesus. Some appear orthodox at first blush which is why knowing the Bible for yourself is so important. Record below what you learn but don't over-do this section. The best way to guard against error is by focusing on truth.

Islam

Church of Jesus Christ of Latter Day Saints (Mormonism)

Jehovah's Witnesses

Hinduism

Buddism

Other

FYI:

Four Accounts, One Gospel
Matthew, Mark, Luke, and John give four separate accounts of the one Gospel of Jesus Christ. Gospel comes from the Greek word *euaggelion* which means "good news."

FYI:

Start with Prayer
You've probably heard it before and if we study together in the future, you're sure to hear it again. Whenever you read or study God's Word, first pray and ask His Spirit to be your Guide. Jesus says that the Spirit will lead us into all truth.

JESUS
SWEETEST NAME I KNOW

WHO JESUS IS AND WHY IT MATTERS

An Inductive Study of Christology

FLASHBACK: "From the Foundation of the World"

Every year at Christmas we celebrate the incarnation of Jesus Christ, His taking on flesh and blood and becoming one of us. We're going to look closely at the Gospel accounts and various New Testament Christological passages as we consider how long Jesus has existed.

We're going to begin with some theologically packed verses. At this point, though, our main focus will be on time. Let's set our framework by asking and answering a variety of "When?" questions.

OBSERVE the TEXT of SCRIPTURE

READ the following passages and **CIRCLE** every reference to *before the foundation of the world (pro kataboles kosmou)*. The first text quotes Jesus. The speaker in the second text is Paul, in the third, Peter.

John 17:1-2, 24

1 *Jesus spoke these things; and lifting up His eyes to heaven, He said, "Father, the hour has come; glorify Your Son, that the Son may glorify You,*

2 *even as You gave Him authority over all flesh, that to all whom You have given Him, He may give eternal life."*

24 *"Father, I desire that they also, whom You have given Me, be with Me where I am, so that they may see My glory which You have given Me, for You loved Me before the foundation of the world."*

Ephesians 1:2-4

2 *Grace to you and peace from God our Father and the Lord Jesus Christ.*

3 *Blessed be the God and Father of our Lord Jesus Christ, who has blessed us with every spiritual blessing in the heavenly places in Christ,*

4 *just as He chose us in Him before the foundation of the world, that we would be holy and blameless before Him.*

1 Peter 1:17-21

17 *If you address as Father the One who impartially judges according to each one's work, conduct yourselves in fear during the time of your stay on earth;*

18 *knowing that you were not redeemed with perishable things like silver or gold from your futile way of life inherited from your forefathers,*

19 *but with precious blood, as of a lamb unblemished and spotless, the blood of Christ.*

20 *For He was foreknown before the foundation of the world, but has appeared in these last times for the sake of you*

21 *who through Him are believers in God, who raised Him from the dead and gave Him glory, so that your faith and hope are in God.*

FYI:

Reading the Context

From time to time in our study we'll cross-reference Scripture to see what other passages say about a similar topic. On the next couple of pages, for instance, we're going to consider whether Jesus existed prior to His incarnation by examining verses where the phrase *before the foundation of the world* appears.

You can read the verses right here in the workbook but if you have time, you'll benefit by reading the entire chapter to establish contexts for yourself.

JESUS
SWEETEST NAME I KNOW

WHO JESUS IS AND WHY IT MATTERS

An Inductive Study of Christology

DISCUSS with your GROUP or PONDER on your own . . .

What did you initially observe from the texts? How do they compare with one another?

John 17 Questions

Who is Jesus addressing?

What relationship do the two have?

How far back do they go?

Did the Father begin loving Jesus when He was born? When did the Father love Him?

ONE STEP FURTHER:

Reading the Context
If you have some extra time this week, read John 17, Ephesians 1, and 1 Peter 1 to see the contexts of the verses we're looking at. Jot down your observations below.

John 17

Ephesians 1

1 Peter 1

JESUS
SWEETEST NAME I KNOW

WHO JESUS IS AND WHY IT MATTERS

An Inductive Study of Christology

Ephesians 1 Questions

What does Paul say happened "before the foundation of the world"?

Who is the "He" who chose?

What does "in Christ" (vv. 3 and 4) mean?

1 Peter Questions

How are people redeemed?

When did Christ appear on earth?

Is this when God's plan started? Explain.

Summary Questions

What existed "before the foundation of the world"? What happened then?

What does this have to do with the person and work of Jesus Christ?

What, if any, implications does this have for you?

Looking at Jesus "before the foundation of the world" provides a good foundation for our study but there is so much more about pre-Christmas Jesus throughout the pages of Scripture. Let's look at three more passages pointing to His work in creation.

OBSERVE the TEXT of SCRIPTURE

READ the following texts and **CIRCLE** any time phrases (*before, in the beginning,* etc.). **UNDERLINE** any words or phrases related to creation (*creation, created, came into being,* etc.).

Colossians 1:15-17

15 He [Jesus] is the image of the invisible God, the firstborn of all creation.

16 For by Him all things were created, both in the heavens and on earth, visible and invisible, whether thrones or dominions or rulers or authorities—all things have been created through Him and for Him.

17 He is before all things, and in Him all things hold together.

JESUS
SWEETEST NAME I KNOW

WHO JESUS IS AND WHY IT MATTERS

An Inductive Study of Christology

9

Genesis 1:1-2, 26

1 In the beginning God created the heavens and the earth.

2 The earth was formless and void, and darkness was over the surface of the deep, and the Spirit of God was moving over the surface of the waters.

26 Then God said, "Let Us make man in Our image, according to Our likeness; and let them rule over the fish of the sea and over the birds of the sky and over the cattle and over all the earth, and over every creeping thing that creeps on the earth."

John 1:1-3, 14

1 In the beginning was the Word, and the Word was with God, and the Word was God.

2 He was in the beginning with God.

3 All things came into being through Him, and apart from Him nothing came into being that has come into being.

14 And the Word became flesh, and dwelt among us, and we saw His glory, glory as of the only begotten from the Father, full of grace and truth.

ONE STEP FURTHER:

Reading the Context

Again, if you have time, invest some reading the contexts. Jot down your observations from Colossians 1, Genesis 1, and John 1.

Colossians 1

Genesis 1

John 1

DISCUSS with your GROUP or PONDER on your own . . .

What did you initially observe from the texts?

Questions on Colossians

What do these verses tell us about Jesus?

What do they tell us about what Jesus did and does?

JESUS
SWEETEST NAME I KNOW

WHO JESUS IS AND WHY IT MATTERS

An Inductive Study of Christology

Do you have any follow-up questions for this text you'd like to pursue? If so, what?

Questions on Genesis and John

According to Genesis, who created the heavens and earth?

Is anyone else mentioned in these Genesis verses? If so, who?

Is "the Spirit of God" (v. 2) "God" (v. 1)? Explain your answer.

According to John who or what "was" in the beginning?

JESUS
SWEETEST NAME I KNOW

WHO JESUS IS AND WHY IT MATTERS

An Inductive Study of Christology

How does John 1:1-3 describe the Word?

How does John 1:14 expand the definition?

Summary Questions

What do these texts tell us about Christ before Christmas?

What do they tell us about Christ after Christmas, about His role in the universe today?

Why does this matter?

THE QUESTION AT HAND . . .

As we close our first week of study, let's look again at the question Jesus posed to Peter. It is the question He asks every person to answer: *Who do you say that I am?*

OBSERVE the TEXT of SCRIPTURE

READ Matthew 16:13-17 and **MARK** every reference to *Jesus*.

Matthew 16:13-17

13 *Now when Jesus came into the district of Caesarea Philippi, He was asking His disciples, "Who do people say that the Son of Man is?"*

14 *And they said, "Some say John the Baptist; and others, Elijah; but still others, Jeremiah, or one of the prophets."*

15 *He said to them, "But who do you say that I am?"*

16 *Simon Peter answered, "You are the Christ, the Son of the living God."*

17 *And Jesus said to him, "Blessed are you, Simon Barjona, because flesh and blood did not reveal this to you, but My Father who is in heaven.*

DISCUSS with your GROUP or PONDER on your own . . .

How does Jesus refer to Himself here?

Who do other people think He is?

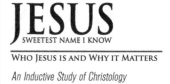

JESUS
SWEETEST NAME I KNOW

WHO JESUS IS AND WHY IT MATTERS

An Inductive Study of Christology

> **FYI:**
>
> **Two Caesareas**
> From time to time we run into biblical cities with the same name. Simon Peter confessed Jesus as the Christ at Caesarea Philippi, a city near the source of the Jordan River—over 20 miles north of the Sea of Galilee. Phillip the tetrarch named the city in honor of Augustus Caesar.
>
> The other Caesarea, also named for Augustus, was a major port city located on the coast of the Mediterranean Sea.

Week One: **Who Do You Say I Am?**

How does Peter answer the question: "But who do you say that I am?"

What does the word *Christ* mean? What was Peter declaring about Jesus?

Where did he get this information?

How do people today know who Jesus is? Can we argue people to Jesus? Explain and cite Scripture to support your view.

WHO JESUS IS AND WHY IT MATTERS

An Inductive Study of Christology

Digging Deeper

Matthew, Mark, Luke, and John

While we'll be all over the Bible during our study together, we'll spend much time in the Gospels looking at Jesus. If you have some extra time this week, look for background information on the Gospel writers. Who were they? What primary audience was each addressing? Which Gospel accounts have the most in common? Is any one of them a stand-alone? Record background information on the Gospels and their writers below.

Matthew

Mark

FYI:

Too open-ended?

My goal with open-ended questions—particularly in **Digging Deeper** sections—is to challenge you to think for yourself without depending on prompts. Over time this will help you reason through texts more and more for yourself. I believe you'll discover more if you're given more room to ask questions and explore.

Luke

John

Notes

@THE END OF THE DAY . . .

We have many miles yet to travel in our investigation of Jesus, many other aspects of His person and work to consider. As we close this week of study, take some time to read back through the Scriptures we've looked at and ask God to plant these truths in your heart. Then record below the most important truth about Jesus that you either learned or have been reminded of this week.

Who is this Son of David?

The record of the genealogy of Jesus the Messiah, the son of David, the son of Abraham . . .
—Matthew 1:1

It's easy to look at the Gospel of Matthew from a western Christian perspective and ask, "Why on earth would anyone start off with a genealogy?" But considering the enormity of the question the Old Testament leaves unresolved—"Who is this Son of David?"—there is no better opening line for Matthew's Gospel account.

Matthew, a Jewish man who views Jesus as the fulfillment of Old Testament promises, writes with Jewish readers in mind, making heavy use of both Old Testament quotations and distinctively Jewish phrases such as "the kingdom of heaven" and "Son of David."

First-century Jews believed the coming Messiah would descend from Abraham and David and that His throne and kingdom would endure forever! Matthew lays his cards on the table from the start using Old Testament quotations to teach his audience that the Messiah has come and His name is Jesus!

WHO JESUS IS AND WHY IT MATTERS

An Inductive Study of Christology

Notes

ONE STEP FURTHER:

God's Covenant with David and Others

The Davidic Covenant stands in a line of other covenants in the Bible. In it God promises David a house and throne that will last forever. This "forever house" is deduced from the descendant's permanent rule on the throne. This is not the first time God has covenanted with man. Prior to this, God established covenants with Noah, Abraham, and the nation of Israel (through Moses). If you have some extra time this week, see what you can discover about each of these covenants and record your findings below.

Noahic

Abrahamic

Mosaic

FYI:

A New Covenant to Come

"But this is the covenant which I will make with the house of Israel after those days," declares the LORD, "I will put My law within them and on their heart I will write it; and I will be their God, and they shall be My people. They will not teach again, each man his neighbor and each man his brother, saying, 'Know the LORD,' for they will all know Me, from the least of them to the greatest of them," declares the LORD, "for I will forgive their iniquity, and their sin I will remember no more."

—Jeremiah 31:33-34

JESUS
SWEETEST NAME I KNOW

WHO JESUS IS AND WHY IT MATTERS

An Inductive Study of Christology

REMEMBERING

Take a few minutes to summarize what you learned about Jesus last week.

SETTING the SCENE

Matthew ties Jesus directly to Old Testament prophecy with the phrase "Son of David." While the significance is often lost on modern readers, it was clearly understood by the first-century Jewish audience looking for the prophesied Deliverer.

In order to understand what they were expecting, let's look at 2 Samuel 7 to see the covenant God made with David. We'll jump into the text after David declares his desire to build a permanent house for God. As it turns out, David is in for quite a surprise.

OBSERVE the TEXT of SCRIPTURE

READ 2 Samuel 7:4-29 and **CIRCLE** every occurrence of *house*. **UNDERLINE** every time reference to the future (*forever, endure,* etc.)

2 Samuel 7:4-29

4 *But in the same night the word of the LORD came to Nathan, saying,*

5 *"Go and say to My servant David, 'Thus says the LORD, "Are you the one who should build Me a house to dwell in?*

6 *"For I have not dwelt in a house since the day I brought up the sons of Israel from Egypt, even to this day; but I have been moving about in a tent, even in a tabernacle.*

7 *"Wherever I have gone with all the sons of Israel, did I speak a word with one of the tribes of Israel, which I commanded to shepherd My people Israel, saying, 'Why have you not built Me a house of cedar?' " '*

8 *"Now therefore, thus you shall say to My servant David, 'Thus says the LORD of hosts, "I took you from the pasture, from following the sheep, to be ruler over My people Israel.*

9 *"I have been with you wherever you have gone and have cut off all your enemies from before you; and I will make you a great name, like the names of the great men who are on the earth.*

10 *"I will also appoint a place for My people Israel and will plant them, that they may live in their own place and not be disturbed again, nor will the wicked afflict them any more as formerly,*

11 *even from the day that I commanded judges to be over My people Israel; and I will give you rest from all your enemies. The LORD also declares to you that the LORD will make a house for you.*

12 *"When your days are complete and you lie down with your fathers, I will raise up your descendant after you, who will come forth from you, and I will establish his kingdom.*

13 *"He shall build a house for My name, and I will establish the throne of his kingdom forever.*

14 *"I will be a father to him and he will be a son to Me; when he commits iniquity, I will correct him with the rod of men and the strokes of the sons of men,*

15 *but My lovingkindness shall not depart from him, as I took it away from Saul, whom I removed from before you.*

16 *"Your house and your kingdom shall endure before Me forever; your throne shall be established forever." ' "*

17 *In accordance with all these words and all this vision, so Nathan spoke to David.*

18 *Then David the king went in and sat before the LORD, and he said, "Who am I, O Lord GOD, and what is my house, that You have brought me this far?*

19 *"And yet this was insignificant in Your eyes, O Lord GOD, for You have spoken also of the house of Your servant concerning the distant future. And this is the custom of man, O Lord GOD.*

20 *"Again what more can David say to You? For You know Your servant, O Lord GOD!*

21 *"For the sake of Your word, and according to Your own heart, You have done all this greatness to let Your servant know.*

22 *"For this reason You are great, O Lord GOD; for there is none like You, and there is no God besides You, according to all that we have heard with our ears.*

23 *"And what one nation on the earth is like Your people Israel, whom God went to redeem for Himself as a people and to make a name for Himself, and to do a great thing for You and awesome things for Your land, before Your people whom You have redeemed for Yourself from Egypt, from nations and their gods?*

24 *"For You have established for Yourself Your people Israel as Your own people forever, and You, O LORD, have become their God.*

INDUCTIVE FOCUS:

What is a key word?

A key word or phrase unlocks the meaning of a text. Key words are usually repeated and are critical to understanding texts.

In 2 Samuel 7, *house* is clearly a key word but there are others. Did you notice any of them? If so, record them below as well as what you learned.

If not, read back through the text watching for words that cluster within a few verses and make sense of the text. If you don't see them right away, don't worry. I'll help by pointing out some as we go.

Identifying key words is a skill that develops over time, but you practice by observing carefully so keep your eyes opened. You will get it; just keep praying and keep looking.

JESUS
SWEETEST NAME I KNOW

WHO JESUS IS AND WHY IT MATTERS

An Inductive Study of Christology

21

25 *"Now therefore, O LORD God, the word that You have spoken concerning Your servant and his house, confirm it forever, and do as You have spoken,*

26 *that Your name may be magnified forever, by saying, 'The LORD of hosts is God over Israel'; and may the house of Your servant David be established before You.*

27 *"For You, O LORD of hosts, the God of Israel, have made a revelation to Your servant, saying, 'I will build you a house'; therefore Your servant has found courage to pray this prayer to You.*

28 *"Now, O Lord GOD, You are God, and Your words are truth, and You have promised this good thing to Your servant.*

29 *"Now therefore, may it please You to bless the house of Your servant, that it may continue forever before You. For You, O Lord GOD, have spoken; and with Your blessing may the house of Your servant be blessed forever."*

DISCUSS with your GROUP or PONDER on your own . . .

What are your initial observations on the text?

What does David want to do for God? Has God ever asked David or anyone else to do this? Does He need anything from David? Explain.

What has God done for David up to this point? What are His plans for Israel?

WHO JESUS IS AND WHY IT MATTERS

An Inductive Study of Christology

What kind of house will God build for David?

Who will build a house for the LORD's name? (Answer directly from the text.)

Whose kingdom will God establish? How long will it last?

Is this descendant Solomon? Why/why not?

When Matthew wrote, Israel clearly did not have a descendant of David occupying an eternal throne. Solomon built a physical temple for God but died. The promises in 2 Samuel were partially fulfilled in David's immediate descendants but Matthew begins his Gospel introducing Jesus as *the* predicted Son of David, the Jewish Messiah, the Savior of the world.

OBSERVE the TEXT of SCRIPTURE

READ Matthew 1 in your Bible. Then, in the excerpted verses below, **CIRCLE** *Son of David* and other references to *Jesus*.

Matthew 1:1-2, 16-23

1 *The record of the genealogy of Jesus the Messiah, the son of David, the son of Abraham:*

2 *Abraham was the father of Isaac, Isaac the father of Jacob, and Jacob the father of Judah and his brothers.*

ONE STEP FURTHER:

Word Study: Messiah

If you have some extra time this week, find the Greek word for *Messiah*—then see if you can find the Hebrew word it corresponds to. What is the literal meaning of the word? Who else is it applied to in the Old Testament? Record your findings below.

JESUS
SWEETEST NAME I KNOW

WHO JESUS IS AND WHY IT MATTERS

An Inductive Study of Christology

Week Two: **Who is this Son of David?**

16 Jacob was the father of Joseph the husband of Mary, by whom Jesus was born, who is called the Messiah.

17 So all the generations from Abraham to David are fourteen generations; from David to the deportation to Babylon, fourteen generations; and from the deportation to Babylon to the Messiah, fourteen generations.

18 Now the birth of Jesus Christ was as follows: when His mother Mary had been betrothed to Joseph, before they came together she was found to be with child by the Holy Spirit.

19 And Joseph her husband, being a righteous man and not wanting to disgrace her, planned to send her away secretly.

20 But when he had considered this, behold, an angel of the Lord appeared to him in a dream, saying, "Joseph, son of David, do not be afraid to take Mary as your wife; for the Child who has been conceived in her is of the Holy Spirit.

21 "She will bear a Son; and you shall call His name Jesus, for He will save His people from their sins."

22 Now all this took place to fulfill what was spoken by the Lord through the prophet:

23 "BEHOLD, THE VIRGIN SHALL BE WITH CHILD AND SHALL BEAR A SON, AND THEY SHALL CALL HIS NAME IMMANUEL," which translated means, "GOD WITH US."

DISCUSS with your GROUP or PONDER on your own . . .

What are your initial observations on the text?

How is Jesus referred to in these verses? How often does Matthew use the term "Messiah"?

ONE STEP FURTHER:

The Women in His Line

If you have some extra time this week, look into the women listed in Jesus' family tree. Who are they? What do other passages of Scripture tell us about their backgrounds? What nationalities do they represent? After you've done your research, record your findings below.

FYI:

Old Testament Quotations

When New Testament authors quote from the Old Testament, the New American Standard Bible puts the quotations in CAPITAL letters. When you see these letters, that's a clue that we're cross-referencing the sources of the quotations.

WHO JESUS IS AND WHY IT MATTERS

An Inductive Study of Christology

What significant covenant lines is Jesus part of according to this genealogy? What did God promise in each of these covenants?

How was Jesus conceived? Why is this significant?

What does the angel say Jesus will do?

What prophet spoke of the virgin birth?

> **FYI:**
>
> **Jesus**
> Jesus in Hebrew is *Yeshua*, which means "Yahweh saves." It is a form of the Old Testament name Joshua.

LOOKING AT THE ORIGINAL PROPHECIES

The Gospels are more widely read than the prophets. In fact, it's likely that you've read the Gospels several times and have not checked out the Old Testament prophecies cited. We're going to do this throughout our study of Matthew.

Remember, Matthew wrote to a primarily Jewish audience. As we look at the Old Testament quotations we'll get a better understanding of how he used these quotes to proclaim Jesus as the Jewish Messiah to the Jewish people.

JESUS
SWEETEST NAME I KNOW

WHO JESUS IS AND WHY IT MATTERS
An Inductive Study of Christology

Week Two: **Who is this Son of David?**

SETTING the SCENE

Matthew tells his readers that the virgin birth of Jesus ultimately fulfills a prophecy Isaiah made when Judah's King Ahaz was threatened by the northern kingdom of Israel and its northern neighbor Syria. God told Ahaz to ask Him for a sign that He would deliver Judah. Ahaz refused to ask, already having set his heart on appealing to the super-power of the day, the king of Assyria, for help. Nevertheless, God gave him a sign with a scope that reached further than Ahaz ever could have imagined.

OBSERVE the TEXT of SCRIPTURE

READ Isaiah 7:10-16 and **UNDERLINE** the details of God's sign to King Ahaz.

Isaiah 7:10-16

10   *Then the LORD spoke again to Ahaz, saying,*

11   *"Ask a sign for yourself from the LORD your God; make it deep as Sheol or high as heaven."*

12   *But Ahaz said, "I will not ask, nor will I test the LORD!"*

13   *Then he said, "Listen now, O house of David! Is it too slight a thing for you to try the patience of men, that you will try the patience of my God as well?*

14   *"Therefore the Lord Himself will give you a sign: Behold, a virgin will be with child and bear a son, and she will call His name Immanuel.*

15   *"He will eat curds and honey at the time He knows enough to refuse evil and choose good.*

16   *"For before the boy will know enough to refuse evil and choose good, the land whose two kings you dread will be forsaken."*

DISCUSS with your GROUP or PONDER on your own . . .

What are your initial observations on the text?

What does the LORD tell King Ahaz to do? How does Ahaz respond?

FYI:

Ichabod and Immanuel

The name *Immanuel*—which means "God with us"—paints a compelling picture of a God who is near. Judah (the Southern Kingdom) had lived through the departure of God's glory from Solomon's temple (recorded in Ezekiel 10) prior to their exile to Babylon. Years before that Eli's dying daughter-in-law named her son *Ichabod*, "the glory has departed," when she learned that the Philistines captured God's ark. God's plans, though, were to dwell among His people and in Jesus we see Him doing exactly that, making the way for eternal restoration.

What sign does the LORD give in spite of Ahaz's refusal?

What does God say will happen near-term to the the two kings Ahaz fears?

Viewed in isolation, Isaiah 7:14 can refer to a normal birth. But a virgin marrying and having a child is not a sign "deep as Sheol or high as heaven" (7:11). What *is* remarkable are the subsequent mentions of this child in Isaiah 9 and Isaiah 11 and Matthew's interpretation. Viewed together, these refer to more than a short-term prophetic fulfillment.

JESUS
SWEETEST NAME I KNOW

WHO JESUS IS AND WHY IT MATTERS
An Inductive Study of Christology

OBSERVE the TEXT of SCRIPTURE

READ Isaiah 9:6-7 and Isaiah 11:1-5. **CIRCLE** every reference to the *child* (include all synonyms) and **UNDERLINE** every reference to time (*eternal, no end,* etc.).

Isaiah 9:6-7

6 *For a child will be born to us, a son will be given to us;*
   And the government will rest on His shoulders;
   And His name will be called Wonderful Counselor, Mighty God,
   Eternal Father, Prince of Peace.

7 *There will be no end to the increase of His government or of peace,*
   On the throne of David and over his kingdom,
   To establish it and to uphold it with justice and righteousness
   From then on and forevermore.
   The zeal of the LORD of hosts will accomplish this.

Isaiah 11:1-5

1 *Then a shoot will spring from the stem of Jesse,*
   And a branch from his roots will bear fruit.

2 *The Spirit of the LORD will rest on Him,*
   The spirit of wisdom and understanding,
   The spirit of counsel and strength,
   The spirit of knowledge and the fear of the LORD.

3 *And He will delight in the fear of the LORD,*
   And He will not judge by what His eyes see,
   Nor make a decision by what His ears hear;

4 *But with righteousness He will judge the poor,*
   And decide with fairness for the afflicted of the earth;
   And He will strike the earth with the rod of His mouth,
   And with the breath of His lips He will slay the wicked.

5 *Also righteousness will be the belt about His loins,*
   And faithfulness the belt about His waist.

DISCUSS with your GROUP or PONDER on your own . . .

What are your initial observations from the text?

JESUS
SWEETEST NAME I KNOW

WHO JESUS IS AND WHY IT MATTERS

An Inductive Study of Christology

What additional information does Isaiah 9 give us about the child?

What names will He be called? What significance do these have?

Whose throne will this child sit upon? How long will He reign?

Is this a *mortal* man? Explain.

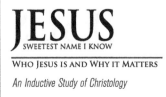

WHO JESUS IS AND WHY IT MATTERS

An Inductive Study of Christology

Digging Deeper

Read the Gospel of Matthew

If you have some extra time this week, start reading the Gospel of Matthew for yourself. Keep a running list of all the names and titles attributed to Jesus as you go and see what you can discover about each.

Who is Jesse and why is he mentioned? (If you don't know, use a concordance to find where he is mentioned in the Bible.)

ONE STEP FURTHER:

Jesse, Samuel, and David's Anointing

If you have some extra time this week read the account of David's anointing in 1 Samuel 16:1-17 to learn more about David's dad, Jesse. Record your findings below.

What imagery does Isaiah 11 use in reference to the Child?

Describe the Child. Specifically, what will characterize Him? What will He do?

We're working through a tremendous amount of content this week, so take a little time right now to reflect on what has been your most significant discovery so far. Record your thoughts below.

JESUS
SWEETEST NAME I KNOW

WHO JESUS IS AND WHY IT MATTERS

An Inductive Study of Christology

OBSERVE the TEXT of SCRIPTURE

READ Matthew 2 carefully for the account of Jesus' birth, the Magi's visit, the flight to Egypt, and the return to Israel. In Matthew 2:4-6 **CIRCLE** every reference to location.

Matthew 2:4-6

4 *Gathering together all the chief priests and scribes of the people, he inquired of them where the Messiah was to be born.*

5 *They said to him, "In Bethlehem of Judea; for this is what has been written by the prophet:*

6 *'AND YOU, BETHLEHEM, LAND OF JUDAH, ARE BY NO MEANS LEAST AMONG THE LEADERS OF JUDAH; FOR OUT OF YOU SHALL COME FORTH A RULER WHO WILL SHEPHERD MY PEOPLE ISRAEL.' "*

DISCUSS with your GROUP or PONDER on your own . . .

Where and when is Jesus born?

Who comes to visit Him and why?

Who is threatened by the birth? Where does he get his information?

According to Matthew 2:6, whose Bethlehem birth was prophesied?

FYI:

Bethlehem

Bethlehem means "house of bread" (*beth* is house, *lechem* is bread). God sent Jesus, the bread of life, to be born of a woman in Bethlehem, the house of bread.

ONE STEP FURTHER:

How did the Magi know about God?

Have you ever wondered why Magi in the East would be looking for a star and how they'd have a clue that it was related to Jesus? God could have revealed something to them directly, but there may be other explanations. Spend some time this week considering this question. Think about people who could have brought word about the one true God to these regions of the earth. Record your thoughts below and support them with Scripture.

Where is Bethlehem in relation to Mary and Joseph's home town? (Check on a Bible map if needed.)

How is Messiah described in the prophet's quotation? What details does the text give?

What prophet is Matthew quoting?

What do we know about the Magi? Who were they? What did they bring? What did they do?

FYI:

The Context of Micah

Micah of Moresheth wrote during the days of Kings Jotham, Ahaz, and Hezekiah of Judah. His prophecies were about coming judgments on both Samaria (the capital of the Northern Kingdom of Israel) and Jerusalem (the capital of the Southern Kingdom of Judah). Judgment looms because both kingdoms have rebelled against God.

Still, in the midst of destruction that will come at the hands of Assyria and Babylon, hope remains in the promise of the Messiah who will one day deliver His people.

FYI:

Nazareth

"Nazareth" appears in each of the four Gospel accounts and twice in the book of Acts and is typically used with reference to Jesus. This small village located south-west of the Sea of Galilee is not mentioned anywhere in the Old Testament but the disciple Philip gives a glimpse into how the Israelites viewed the town when he asked in John 1:45, "Can any good thing come out of Nazareth?"

OBSERVE the TEXT of SCRIPTURE

READ Micah 5 in your Bible. Then in the text below **CIRCLE** every reference to the *One* (including pronouns). **UNDERLINE** every reference to what He will do. Put a **TRIANGLE** over every reference to *God*.

Micah 5:2-6

2 *"But as for you, Bethlehem Ephrathah, too little to be among the clans of Judah, from you One will go forth for Me to be ruler in Israel. His goings forth are from long ago, from the days of eternity."*

3 *Therefore He will give them up until the time when she who is in labor has borne a child. Then the remainder of His brethren will return to the sons of Israel.*

JESUS
SWEETEST NAME I KNOW

WHO JESUS IS AND WHY IT MATTERS

An Inductive Study of Christology

Week Two: **Who is this Son of David?**

4 *And He will arise and shepherd His flock in the strength of the LORD, in the majesty of the name of the LORD His God. And they will remain, because at that time He will be great to the ends of the earth.*

5 *This One will be our peace. When the Assyrian invades our land, when he tramples on our citadels, then we will raise against him seven shepherds and eight leaders of men.*

6 *They will shepherd the land of Assyria with the sword, the land of Nimrod at its entrances; and He will deliver us from the Assyrian when he attacks our land and when he tramples our territory.*

DISCUSS with your GROUP or PONDER on your own . . .

How far back are the "goings forth" of the One who "will go forth"? What will He be in Israel?

What city will He emerge from?

What narrative shift takes place between verses 2 and 3? Who is speaking in verse 2? In verse 3?

Who does the "He" at the beginning of verse 3 refer to?

FYI:

But He Will Be from Bethlehem

Hindsight is said to be 20/20. When we read about Jesus' birth in Bethlehem and about Nazareth being his hometown, it's easy to see how He fulfills Old Testament prophecies of the Messiah coming from Bethlehem. But among those who knew only that He came from Nazareth many assumed He could not be the Messiah. We see this in John 7:41-42 where some, reflecting on Micah's prophecy, say, "Surely the Christ is not going to come from Galilee, is He? Has not the Scripture said that the Christ comes from the descendants of David, and from Bethlehem, the village where David was?"

In light of Matthew 2, who is "she who is in labor"?

What happens in the time between Micah's writing and the child's appearance? Politically what did that mean for the nation?

When the child is born, what will He do?

What will He bring?

What will He do to Israel's enemies?

What parts of this prophecy apply to Jesus? Do any not apply to Him?

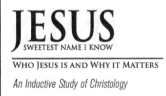

JESUS
SWEETEST NAME I KNOW

WHO JESUS IS AND WHY IT MATTERS

An Inductive Study of Christology

Can you see why Jewish people would be looking for an *earthly* king?

What in the passage points to a different kind of king?

What hope does this king give you?

OBSERVE the TEXT of SCRIPTURE

READ Matthew 2:15, 21-23 and **UNDERLINE** the phrase attributed to "the prophets."

Matthew 2:15, 21-23

15 *He remained there until the death of Herod. This was to fulfill what had been spoken by the Lord through the prophet: "OUT OF EGYPT I CALLED MY SON."*

21 *So Joseph got up, took the Child and His mother, and came into the land of Israel.*

22 *But when he heard that Archelaus was reigning over Judea in place of his father Herod, he was afraid to go there. Then after being warned by God in a dream, he left for the regions of Galilee,*

23 *and came and lived in a city called Nazareth. This was to fulfill what was spoken through the prophets: "He shall be called a Nazarene."*

DISCUSS with your GROUP or PONDER on your own . . .

When Joseph returned to Israel with Jesus and Mary, where did they settle and why?

Explain how Israel, Judea, Galilee and Nazareth relate to one another in terms of where Jesus' family settled.

Are the NASB translators telling us something by not capitalizing the sentence attributed to the prophets?

Take a minute to list some of the challenges Mary and Joseph faced prior to Jesus' birth and in the early years of His life.

How can knowing the way God led them encourage you when you face challenges in your life?

Jesus grew up in a family shamed by people who considered Him conceived "out of wedlock." They were pursued by someone intending to kill Him. They knew dangers, trial, and hardship. The author of Hebrews tells us that Jesus can sympathize with our weaknesses, because He was "tempted in all things as we are, yet without sin" (Hebrews 4:15). He truly is the perfect high priest.

ONE STEP FURTHER:

He Shall Be Called a Nazarene

The sentence "He shall be called a Nazarene" doesn't appear in the Old Testament. If you're up for a challenge this week, see if you can unearth some possibilities of Matthew's source for this prophecy. For this one you'll probably need the help of a commentary or Hebrew word study tool. See what you discover and record your findings below.

Digging Deeper

Jesus and the Exodus Generation

If you have some extra time this week, examine how events in Jesus' life parallel events in Israel's exodus generation. We've already seen one clue to this in Matthew 2's quotation of Hosea 11:1 used first for Israel—"OUT OF EGYPT I CALLED MY SON" (2:15).

How does Israel serve as a type of Jesus? How did Jesus succeed in places where Israel failed? Record your findings below.

FYI:

What is a "type"?
A type is a word in the Old Testament that points to something similar in the New Testament. The person or event—Elijah for example—is called the "type" while the counterpart—in this case John—is the "antitype."

OBSERVE the TEXT of SCRIPTURE

READ Matthew 3 in your Bible noting how Jesus is described and referred to. In Matthew 3:1-4 below, **CIRCLE** every reference to John the Baptist and pronouns that refer to him.

Matthew 3:1-4

1   Now in those days John the Baptist came, preaching in the wilderness of Judea, saying,

2   "Repent, for the kingdom of heaven is at hand."

3   For this is the one referred to by Isaiah the prophet when he said, "THE VOICE OF ONE CRYING IN THE WILDERNESS, 'MAKE READY THE WAY OF THE LORD, MAKE HIS PATHS STRAIGHT!' "

4   Now John himself had a garment of camel's hair and a leather belt around his waist; and his food was locusts and wild honey.

DISCUSS with your GROUP or PONDER on your own . . .

How is the LORD described in Matthew 3? What names and descriptions are given to Him?

Describe John the Baptist.

Who does Matthew say John is?

Does John's clothing allude to other biblical characters? If so, who and how?

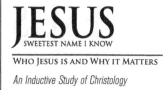

JESUS
SWEETEST NAME I KNOW

WHO JESUS IS AND WHY IT MATTERS

An Inductive Study of Christology

OBSERVE the TEXT of SCRIPTURE

READ Isaiah 40:3-5 and **CIRCLE** every reference to the *LORD*, including synonyms and pronouns.

Isaiah 40:3-5

3 A voice is calling, "Clear the way for the LORD in the wilderness; make smooth in the desert a highway for our God.

4 "Let every valley be lifted up, and every mountain and hill be made low; and let the rough ground become a plain, and the rugged terrain a broad valley;

5 Then the glory of the LORD will be revealed, and all flesh will see it *together*; for the mouth of the LORD has spoken."

ONE STEP FURTHER:

Isaiah 40

If you have time this week, read Isaiah 40 and record what you discover below.

DISCUSS with your GROUP or PONDER on your own . . .

What does the voice in Isaiah call out? How does this compare with what John calls out?

What does the voice say will be revealed? Compare this with what John says about Jesus in John 1:14 and 2:11.

According to Isaiah, who is the highway being smoothed for? If this is a prophecy about Jesus, what does it teach about who He is?

Digging Deeper

John the Baptist and Elijah

The Old Testament closes with these words in Malachi 4:5-6: "Behold, I am going to send you Elijah the prophet before the coming of the great and terrible day of the LORD. He will restore the hearts of the fathers to their children and the hearts of the children to their fathers, so that I will not come and smite the land with a curse." If you have time this week, explore the life of Elijah who was an Old Testament "type" of John the Baptist.

Describe Elijah from the texts of 1 and 2 Kings.

Describe John the Baptist from the Gospel accounts.

How are Elijah and John similar? How are they different?

How is Elijah a type of John? What significance does this have for us as we interpret the text?

FYI:

Your Bible GPS
When you need to find a specific reference in the Bible, an online concordance serves as a biblical GPS system while a traditional concordance is more like a map. For this **DIGGING DEEPER** assignment, type Elijah into an online concordance search engine to find every verse where his name appears in the Bible.

JESUS
SWEETEST NAME I KNOW

WHO JESUS IS AND WHY IT MATTERS

An Inductive Study of Christology

Week Two: **Who is this Son of David?**

A WORD FROM THE FATHER

Jesus' baptism and wilderness temptation that follows mark the beginning of His public ministry.

OBSERVE the TEXT of SCRIPTURE

READ Matthew 3:13-17. Draw a **CROSS** over references to *Jesus* (include pronouns), a **TRIANGLE** over allusions to God the Father (include pronouns) and a **CLOUD** over references to the *Spirit of God*.

Matthew 3:13-17

13 Then Jesus arrived from Galilee at the Jordan coming to John, to be baptized by him.

14 But John tried to prevent Him, saying, "I have need to be baptized by You, and do You come to me?"

15 But Jesus answering said to him, "Permit it at this time; for in this way it is fitting for us to fulfill all righteousness." Then he permitted Him.

16 After being baptized, Jesus came up immediately from the water; and behold, the heavens were opened, and he saw the Spirit of God descending as a dove and lighting on Him,

17 and behold, a voice out of the heavens said, "This is My beloved Son, in whom I am well-pleased."

DISCUSS with your GROUP or PONDER on your own . . .

Does John know who Jesus was? Explain your answer.

Why does John baptize Jesus according to Matthew 3:15?

What has Jesus accomplished at this point in His life?

When Jesus comes up from the water, what happens?

What does the voice from heaven say to Jesus? Whose voice is this?

@THE END OF THE DAY . . .

The past couple of weeks we've been looking at a lot of factual material about Jesus. We've worked through some application questions for sure, but perhaps not as many as we usually do. With that in mind, consider this verse from the author of Hebrews who tells us that the key to not growing weary and losing heart is to continually keep the person and work of Jesus Christ before our eyes: "For consider Him who has endured such hostility by sinners against Himself, so that you will not grow weary and lose heart" (Hebrews 12:3). Before you wrap it up today, what causes you to grow weary and lose heart? What truths about Jesus can help you with this today? Think and pray through these questions and then record your takeaways on the next page.

JESUS
SWEETEST NAME I KNOW

WHO JESUS IS AND WHY IT MATTERS

An Inductive Study of Christology

Week Three
Recognizing the Son of David

All the crowds were amazed, and were saying,
"This man cannot be the Son of David, can he?"
– Matthew 12:23

Jesus' conception, birth, birthplace and other life details fulfilled Old Testament prophecies of the Messiah, the Son who will forever sit on David's throne. The early chapters of Matthew establish an Old Testament basis for Jesus being the Messiah. Still, not everyone who encountered Him recognized Him.

This week we'll look closely at references to Jesus as the Son of David throughout the New Testament. Who recognized Him? Who didn't? What significance did this title have then and now?

JESUS
SWEETEST NAME I KNOW
WHO JESUS IS AND WHY IT MATTERS
An Inductive Study of Christology

Week Three: **Recognizing the Son of David**

Where we are . . .

In chapters 1–3 of his Gospel, Matthew establishes Jesus as the fulfillment of Old Testament prophecy. Jesus' transition to public life and ministry begins with His baptism in Matthew 3 and subsequent temptation by the devil in chapter 4. The devil knows who Jesus is, addressing Him as the Son of God. We'll consider this address a little later in our study.

Matthew 5–7 ("the Sermon on the Mount") is an extended section of Jesus' teaching on the ethics of Kingdom living. We're going to start, after this, with Matthew 8 to look at the "Son of David" references in the New Testament and some Old Testament prophecy along the way!

FYI:

"Son of David" in the New Testament

"Son of David" is used primarily by Matthew in his Gospel although Mark and Luke use it occasionally, typically in passages that parallel Matthew's. Here is the distribution: if you have time, jot down the immediate contexts of each reference.

Matthew:

9:27

12:23

15:22

20:30-31

21:9

21:15

22:42

Mark:

10:47-48

12:35

Luke:

3:31

18:38-39

OBSERVE the TEXT of SCRIPTURE

READ Matthew 8–9 in your Bible paying special attention to the names people use as they address or refer to Jesus. Then in the excerpts below **CIRCLE** every reference to *Jesus* including pronouns and titles *(Son of David, Lord)*.

Matthew 9:26–31

26 This news spread throughout all that land.

27 As Jesus went on from there, two blind men followed Him, crying out, "Have mercy on us, Son of David!"

28 When He entered the house, the blind men came up to Him, and Jesus said to them, "Do you believe that I am able to do this?" They said to Him, "Yes, Lord."

29 Then He touched their eyes, saying, "It shall be done to you according to your faith."

30 And their eyes were opened. And Jesus sternly warned them: "See that no one knows about this!"

31 But they went out and spread the news about Him throughout all that land.

DISCUSS with your GROUP or PONDER on your own . . .

Who addresses Jesus in Matthew 8? What titles do they give Him?

What is Jesus primarily doing in Matthew 8:1-18?

How does Matthew say these actions fulfill Isaiah's prophecy?

Can you relate to Jesus' titles? What, if any, implications does each have as you live a life of obedience to Him? Explain.

In what ways has Jesus healed you?

Who approaches Jesus in Matthew 8:19-34?

What do we learn about Jesus from these interactions?

JESUS
SWEETEST NAME I KNOW

WHO JESUS IS AND WHY IT MATTERS

An Inductive Study of Christology

Notes

Digging Deeper

Messiah Our Healer

Matthew quotes Isaiah 53:4: "HE HIMSELF TOOK OUR INFIRMITIES AND CARRIED AWAY OUR DISEASES." If you have some extra time this week, examine Isaiah 53 to consider the significance of healing as a pointer to the Messiah. Do other Old Testament passages connect the Messiah with healing? Use your concordance and see what you can discover. As you study, also consider what Scripture says about God as Healer.

God as Healer

Messiah as Healer

What conclusions have you drawn about Jesus' healing ministry and its relationship to Old Testament teaching about God and prophecy about the Messiah?

Describe the difference between the disciples' and the demons' understanding of Jesus.

Is believing Jesus is the Son of God enough to save? Explain your answer from Scripture.

What people does Jesus encounter in Matthew 9? What does each want from Him?

Who *sees* Him as the Son of David? What physical condition are they in?

What do these men ask for in Matthew 9:27? How does this compare with Matthew 9:13? (Hint: Look at the Greek words in both texts to see if you find a link.)

What does Jesus do for all the people He interacts with in Matthew 8–9? Why is this significant?

ONE STEP FURTHER:

"Go and learn what this means . . . "

Jesus quotes Hosea 6:6 when he says "I DESIRE COMPASSION, AND NOT SACRIFICE." If you have some extra time this week, examine the context of Hosea and explain the point Jesus is making.

JESUS
SWEETEST NAME I KNOW

WHO JESUS IS AND WHY IT MATTERS

An Inductive Study of Christology

Digging Deeper

The Gospel of the Kingdom

What did the Old Testament say about the Kingdom of God? What Kingdom did Jesus announce? If you have some extra time this week, use your concordance and other study helps to see what you can discover about the Kingdom the Jewish people were looking for. How did Jesus fulfill this? How did people miss it?

The Old Testament expectation:

The Kingdom Jesus announced:

Based on what you've learned, briefly explain how Jesus fulfilled Old Testament prophecy regarding the coming Kingdom of God. As you answer, explain it as simply and clearly as possible.

FYI:

The Synoptic Gospels

Each of the four Gospels recounts the life and times of Jesus Christ. They overlap in the events they report but Matthew, Mark, and Luke do so more regularly than John, so they are referred to as "Synoptic ['same view'] Gospels." I think of them as the triplets and John as the fourth brother who has a different look about him.

JESUS
SWEETEST NAME I KNOW

WHO JESUS IS AND WHY IT MATTERS

An Inductive Study of Christology

OBSERVE the TEXT of SCRIPTURE

READ Matthew 12, then **CIRCLE** every reference to *David* in the excerpt below.
UNDERLINE every reference to *Sabbath*.

Matthew 12:1-23

1   At that time Jesus went through the grainfields on the Sabbath, and His disciples became hungry and began to pick the heads of grain and eat.

2   But when the Pharisees saw this, they said to Him, "Look, Your disciples do what is not lawful to do on a Sabbath."

3   But He said to them, "Have you not read what David did when he became hungry, he and his companions,

4   how he entered the house of God, and they ate the consecrated bread, which was not lawful for him to eat nor for those with him, but for the priests alone?

5   "Or have you not read in the Law, that on the Sabbath the priests in the temple break the Sabbath and are innocent?

6   "But I say to you that something greater than the temple is here.

7   "But if you had known what this means, 'I DESIRE COMPASSION, AND NOT A SACRIFICE,' you would not have condemned the innocent.

8   "For the Son of Man is Lord of the Sabbath."

9   Departing from there, He went into their synagogue.

10   And a man was there whose hand was withered. And they questioned Jesus, asking, "Is it lawful to heal on the Sabbath?"—so that they might accuse Him.

11   And He said to them, "What man is there among you who has a sheep, and if it falls into a pit on the Sabbath, will he not take hold of it and lift it out?

12   "How much more valuable then is a man than a sheep! So then, it is lawful to do good on the Sabbath."

13   Then He said to the man, "Stretch out your hand!" He stretched it out, and it was restored to normal, like the other.

14   But the Pharisees went out and conspired against Him, as to how they might destroy Him.

15   But Jesus, aware of this, withdrew from there. Many followed Him, and He healed them all,

16   and warned them not to tell who He was.

17   This was to fulfill what was spoken through Isaiah the prophet:

18   "BEHOLD, MY SERVANT WHOM I HAVE CHOSEN;
      MY BELOVED IN WHOM MY SOUL is WELL-PLEASED;
      I WILL PUT MY SPIRIT UPON HIM,
      AND HE SHALL PROCLAIM JUSTICE TO THE GENTILES.

19   "HE WILL NOT QUARREL, NOR CRY OUT;
      NOR WILL ANYONE HEAR HIS VOICE IN THE STREETS.

JESUS
SWEETEST NAME I KNOW

WHO JESUS IS AND WHY IT MATTERS

An Inductive Study of Christology

Week Three: **Recognizing the Son of David**

20 *"A BATTERED REED HE WILL NOT BREAK OFF,*
    AND A SMOLDERING WICK HE WILL NOT PUT OUT,
    UNTIL HE LEADS JUSTICE TO VICTORY.

21 *"AND IN HIS NAME THE GENTILES WILL HOPE."*

22 *Then a demon-possessed man who was blind and mute was brought to*
    Jesus, and He healed him, so that the mute man spoke and saw.

23 *All the crowds were amazed, and were saying, "This man cannot be the Son*
    of David, can he?"

ONE STEP FURTHER:

Matthew's Quotes

Matthew quotes heavily from the Old Testament, sometimes citing sources (12:18-21), other times alluding to them (12:7). This week, see if you can find the Isaiah passage Matthew quotes. There are different ways to go about this. You can search on a phrase from the quoted text in a concordance. You can consult a commentary. You can even use Google but make sure you carefully discern the results. As tools change and technologies advance, remember, there is typically more than one way to find the information you're looking for. Record the specific reference in Isaiah that Matthew quotes and any additional observations you have from the text or its context.

DISCUSS with your GROUP or PONDER on your own . . .

What are Jesus and His disciples doing at the beginning of Matthew 12?

Why does this bother the Pharisees?

How does Jesus respond to their accusations? What does He ask them?

What historical people and situations does he refer them to?

What does Jesus say He is greater than?

How does He evidence this?

What affect does this have on the Pharisees?

How does the Pharisees' reaction contrast with the prophecies about the Gentiles?

What does the Isaiah passage say with regard to the Gentiles?

What do the amazed crowds ask in Matthew 12:23?

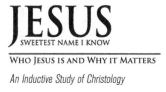

Where we are . . .

By the second half of Matthew 12 the crowds are wondering if Jesus is the prophesied Son of David but the Pharisees claim He casts out demons because He works for the devil. Matthew 12 ends with Jesus speaking out against the scribes and Pharisees who demand a sign. While godless Ninevites responded to Jonah's preaching and the Queen of Sheba sought out Solomon's wisdom, these Israelite leaders are blindly missing God Himself in their midst.

In the span from Matthew 13 to the middle of Matthew 15, Jesus preaches parables of the kingdom, Herod executes John the Baptist, Jesus feeds 5,000 Israelites, and Peter walks on water. At the water-walking event, the disciples in the boat realize Jesus is God's Son—but that's a topic for another chapter.

In the region of Gennesaret, Jesus heals more people as the locals recognize Him and bring their sick to Him.

OBSERVE the TEXT of SCRIPTURE

READ Matthew 15 keeping in mind that the last time we were informed about their whereabouts Jesus and his disciples were in Gennesaret. In Matthew 15:21-31 below, **CIRCLE** *Son of David* and every title given to Jesus. **UNDERLINE** every reference to the woman.

Matthew 15:21-31

21 *Jesus went away from there, and withdrew into the district of Tyre and Sidon.*

22 *And a Canaanite woman from that region came out and* began *to cry out, saying, "Have mercy on me, Lord, Son of David; my daughter is cruelly demon-possessed."*

23 *But He did not answer her a word. And His disciples came and implored Him, saying, "Send her away, because she keeps shouting at us."*

24 *But He answered and said, "I was sent only to the lost sheep of the house of Israel."*

25 *But she came and* began *to bow down before Him, saying, "Lord, help me!"*

26 *And He answered and said, "It is not good to take the children's bread and throw it to the dogs."*

27 *But she said, "Yes, Lord; but even the dogs feed on the crumbs which fall from their masters' table."*

28 *Then Jesus said to her, "O woman, your faith is great; it shall be done for you as you wish." And her daughter was healed at once.*

29 *Departing from there, Jesus went along by the Sea of Galilee, and having gone up on the mountain, He was sitting there.*

30 *And large crowds came to Him, bringing with them those who were lame, crippled, blind, mute, and many others, and they laid them down at His feet; and He healed them.*

31 *So the crowd marveled as they saw the mute speaking, the crippled restored, and the lame walking, and the blind seeing; and they glorified the God of Israel.*

DISCUSS with your GROUP or PONDER on your own . . .

Where is Jesus as Matthew 15 opens?

Who comes to see Him? Where are these people from? What is their nationality?

What prophecy from Isaiah does Jesus refer to regarding these men?

Are these people from God's nation actually God's people? Do they know God? Explain your answer.

Where do Jesus and His disciples go according to verse 21? Where is this?

ONE STEP FURTHER:

Compare the Accounts

If you have time this week, compare Matthew's account of the Canaanite woman with the account that Mark records in Mark 7:24-30. Record your observations below.

Describe the disciples from Matthew 15:21-31 taking into consideration what Jesus says about Israel. Also consider their behavior. Given everything together, how would you sum up the picture? Positive? Negative? Mixed? Explain your answer.

ONE STEP FURTHER:

Word Study: Help!

If you have some time this week, find the Greek word the Canaanite woman uses when she asks Jesus for help. Where else is it used in the New Testament and how is it typically used? Record your findings below.

Describe the woman in Matthew 15:21-31.

How does the woman address Jesus? What does she know?

What does she ask Jesus for first? Compare this with Matthew 9:13 and 12:7. (Be sure to check your Strong numbers!)

FYI:

We Don't Know the Tone

Before you get distressed at the account of Jesus and the Canaanite woman, remember we can't hear the tone of His voice, we can't see the look in His eyes. What is recorded, though, is enough. Jesus gives the woman an opportunity to show her great faith in front of the disciples . . . and she does! He gives her the "bread" she asks for and then physical bread to 4,000+ in a largely Gentile region!

What does the woman realize that the Pharisees have missed?

What do the disciples want Jesus to do that He doesn't do?

JESUS
SWEETEST NAME I KNOW

WHO JESUS IS AND WHY IT MATTERS

An Inductive Study of Christology

Who has correct vision in this scenario? The woman? Jesus? The disciples? Explain.

If you were one of the disciples begging Jesus to send the woman away, what lesson would you have learned that day?

What are Jesus' final words to the woman? Does she get what she came for?

How does the woman compare with the Jewish religious leaders?

Immediately after the incident with the Canaanite woman, where does Jesus go? Which side of the Sea of Galilee is He on? Describe the crowd following Him (v. 31). What hint does verse 31 give us?

What miracle does Jesus do? How many people are involved? Describe them.

ONE STEP FURTHER:

Great Faith/Little Faith

Who else did Jesus say had great faith? Who did He say had little faith? Record your findings and references below. What do you make of this?

Week Three: **Recognizing the Son of David**

Digging Deeper

Zacharias on Jesus

If you have some extra time this week, explore what Zacharias, John the Baptist's dad, said about Jesus in Luke 1:67-79. What did he say about Jesus as the Son of David? What did he expect Him to do to fulfill Old Testament prophecy? What role will his own son, John, play in the unfolding of God's redemptive plan?

Facts about Jesus:

Old Testament prophecies He fulfilled:

John's role:

God's purpose:

Where we are . . .

According to Matthew 15:39 Jesus and His disciples go to the region of Magadan where they again speak to the Pharisees and Sadducees. Midway through chapter 16, Jesus takes the disciples north about 25 miles to Caesarea Philippi, a town long-associated with idol worship. There Peter makes his great Christological confession, "You are the Christ, the Son of the living God." Matthew 17 features Jesus' transfiguration and meeting with Moses and Elijah on a mountain and God confirms Peter's confession with: "This is My beloved Son, with whom I am well-pleased; listen to Him!" More on this later!

In Matthew 18 Jesus explains that humility is the way to greatness in His Kingdom and then tells two parables: about a missing sheep and a king settling accounts.

By Matthew 19, Jesus leaves Galilee and goes south and east to the region of Judea on the other side of the Jordan River. Crowds follow Him and the Pharisees chase after Him to test Him. He fields questions on topics ranging from divorce to eternal life.

As Matthew 20 opens, Jesus tells another kingdom parable about a landowner who hires men to work in his field. As He and His disciples return from beyond the Jordan and travel up toward Jerusalem, He tells them that He will die and be raised from the dead. Still looking for an earthly kingdom, the mother of James and John asks for her sons to sit at Jesus' right and left hands in the kingdom. As they leave Jericho on their way to Jerusalem, Jesus and the disciples encounter two blind men who, like the Canaanite woman, have spiritual sight.

OBSERVE the TEXT of SCRIPTURE

READ Matthew 20:29–Matthew 21:16 and in the section below, **CIRCLE** *Son of David* and every reference to Jesus including pronouns. **UNDERLINE** every reference to the blind men.

Matthew 20:29–34 (see also Luke 18:35-43; Mark 10:46-52; 11:7-10)

29 As they were leaving Jericho, a large crowd followed Him.

30 And two blind men sitting by the road, hearing that Jesus was passing by, cried out, "Lord, have mercy on us, Son of David!"

31 The crowd sternly told them to be quiet, but they cried out all the more, "Lord, Son of David, have mercy on us!"

32 And Jesus stopped and called them, and said, "What do you want Me to do for you?"

33 They said to Him, "Lord, we want our eyes to be opened."

34 Moved with compassion, Jesus touched their eyes; and immediately they regained their sight and followed Him.

Matthew 21:1-16

1 When they had approached Jerusalem and had come to Bethphage, at the Mount of Olives, then Jesus sent two disciples,

ONE STEP FURTHER:

Check Out Luke and Mark
If you have some spare time this week check out these parallel accounts of Luke (18:35-43) and Mark (10:46-52, 11:7-10). Record your findings below.

FYI:

More Signs of the Messianic Age
On that day the deaf will hear words of a book, and out of their gloom and darkness the eyes of the blind will see.

The afflicted also will increase their gladness in the LORD, and the needy of mankind will rejoice in the Holy One of Israel.

—Isaiah 29:18-19

Then the eyes of the blind will be opened and the ears of the deaf will be unstopped. Then the lame will leap like a deer and the tongue of the mute will shout for joy. For waters will break forth in the wilderness and streams in the Arabah.

—Isaiah 35:5-6

JESUS
SWEETEST NAME I KNOW

WHO JESUS IS AND WHY IT MATTERS
An Inductive Study of Christology

Week Three: **Recognizing the Son of David**

ONE STEP FURTHER:

Zechariah 9:9-10

Rejoice greatly, O daughter of Zion! Shout in triumph, O daughter of Jerusalem! Behold, your king is coming to you; He is just and endowed with salvation, humble, and mounted on a donkey, even on a colt, the foal of a donkey. I will cut off the chariot from Ephraim and the horse from Jerusalem; and the bow of war will be cut off. And He will speak peace to the nations; and His dominion will be from sea to sea, and from the River to the ends of the earth.

—Zechariah 9:9-10

If you have time this week, read the rest of Zechariah 9 for the context of this quotation and record your observations below.

2 saying to them, "Go into the village opposite you, and immediately you will find a donkey tied there and a colt with her; untie them and bring them to Me.

3 "If anyone says anything to you, you shall say, 'The Lord has need of them,' and immediately he will send them."

4 This took place to fulfill what was spoken through the prophet:

5 "SAY TO THE DAUGHTER OF ZION,
'BEHOLD YOUR KING IS COMING TO YOU,
GENTLE, AND MOUNTED ON A DONKEY,
EVEN ON A COLT, THE FOAL OF A BEAST OF BURDEN.' "

6 The disciples went and did just as Jesus had instructed them,

7 and brought the donkey and the colt, and laid their coats on them; and He sat on the coats.

8 Most of the crowd spread their coats in the road, and others were cutting branches from the trees and spreading them in the road.

9 The crowds going ahead of Him, and those who followed, were shouting,
"Hosanna to the Son of David;
BLESSED IS HE WHO COMES IN THE NAME OF THE LORD;
Hosanna in the highest!"

10 When He had entered Jerusalem, all the city was stirred, saying, "Who is this?"

11 And the crowds were saying, "This is the prophet Jesus, from Nazareth in Galilee."

12 And Jesus entered the temple and drove out all those who were buying and selling in the temple, and overturned the tables of the money changers and the seats of those who were selling doves.

13 And He said to them, "It is written, 'MY HOUSE SHALL BE CALLED A HOUSE OF PRAYER'; but you are making it a ROBBERS' DEN."

14 And the blind and the lame came to Him in the temple, and He healed them.

15 But when the chief priests and the scribes saw the wonderful things that He had done, and the children who were shouting in the temple, "Hosanna to the Son of David," they became indignant

16 and said to Him, "Do You hear what these children are saying?" And Jesus said to them, "Yes; have you never read, 'OUT OF THE MOUTH OF INFANTS AND NURSING BABIES YOU HAVE PREPARED PRAISE FOR YOURSELF'?"

DISCUSS with your GROUP or PONDER on your own . . .

What does Jesus tell His disciples as they go up to Jerusalem? Be specific.

Compare James and John's mom with the two blind men. How does each approach Jesus?

What question does Jesus ask each of them? What do they ask Him for?

What do the questions reveal about the people who asked them?

How do these blind men compare with the blind men in Matthew 8 and the Canaanite woman in Matthew 15?

ONE STEP FURTHER:

Psalm 118 and Psalm 8

O LORD, do save, we beseech You; O LORD, we beseech You, do send prosperity! Blessed is the one who comes in the name of the LORD; we have blessed you from the house of the LORD.
                    —Psalm 118:25-26

O LORD, our Lord, how majestic is Your name in all the earth, Who have displayed Your splendor above the heavens! From the mouth of infants and nursing babes You have established strength because of Your adversaries, to make the enemy and the revengeful cease.
                    —Psalm 8:1-2

If you have extra time this week, read the full Psalms for the contexts and record your observations below.

JESUS
SWEETEST NAME I KNOW
WHO JESUS IS AND WHY IT MATTERS
An Inductive Study of Christology

Week Three: **Recognizing the Son of David**

When Jesus enters Jerusalem, what prophecies does He fulfill?

How do the people address Jesus as He enters the city?

How do the crowds coming into the city treat Jesus?

How does this compare with those who are from the city? What is their hesitation?

How do these views compare with today's? How do you treat Jesus? How does your culture treat Him?

Does it matter? Why?

Where we are . . .

Matthew 21 closes with a question about authority and more kingdom parables which anger the Pharisees and other religious leaders. Matthew 22 opens with Jesus' parable of the wedding feast, Pharisees trying to trap Him with a tax-evasion question, and Sadducees questioning resurrection and afterlife with the vexing problem of multiple marriages. In Matthew 22:41ff Jesus turns questions back on the Pharisees as He pushes the point that He is *the* Son of David.

OBSERVE the TEXT of SCRIPTURE

READ Matthew 22:41-46 and **CIRCLE** every reference to *Jesus*. **UNDERLINE** every reference to *David* and put a **TRIANGLE** over every reference to God (you're looking for the "Lord" in the text that refers to God the Father).

Matthew 22:41-46 (also Mark 12:35-37)

41 *Now while the Pharisees were gathered together, Jesus asked them a question:*

42 *"What do you think about the Christ, whose son is He?" They said to Him, "The son of David."*

43 *He said to them, "Then how does David in the Spirit call Him 'Lord,' saying,*

44 *'THE LORD SAID TO MY LORD,
"SIT AT MY RIGHT HAND,
UNTIL I PUT YOUR ENEMIES BENEATH YOUR FEET" '?*

45 *"If David then calls Him 'Lord,' how is He his son?"*

46 *No one was able to answer Him a word, nor did anyone dare from that day on to ask Him another question.*

DISCUSS with your GROUP or PONDER on your own . . .

How does Jesus engage the Pharisees? Explain His line of questioning.

How does it work? How do the Pharisees respond?

Notes

ONE STEP FURTHER:

**Psalm 110–
A Psalm of David**

1 The LORD says to my Lord: "Sit at My right hand until I make Your enemies a footstool for Your feet."

2 The LORD will stretch forth Your strong scepter from Zion, saying, "Rule in the midst of Your enemies."

3 Your people will volunteer freely in the day of Your power; in holy array, from the womb of the dawn, Your youth are to You as the dew.

4 The LORD has sworn and will not change His mind, "You are a priest forever according to the order of Melchizedek."

5 The Lord is at Your right hand; He will shatter kings in the day of His wrath.

6 He will judge among the nations, He will fill them with corpses, He will shatter the chief men over a broad country.

7 He will drink from the brook by the wayside; therefore He will lift up His head.

If you have some extra time, see how the author of Hebrews also uses this Psalm in reference to Jesus and record your observations below.

WHO JESUS IS AND WHY IT MATTERS

An Inductive Study of Christology

Digging Deeper

The Other "Son of David" Phrases

Son of David is clearly a high-frequency title for Jesus in the book of Matthew as we've seen in our study this week. Matthew drives home Jesus as the heir to David's throne time and time again. He is not the only one concerned with this title, however. Jesus is called the Son of David in both John's Gospel and Revelation. Peter, Paul, and James give Him this title in the Acts of the Apostles. If you have some extra time this week, explore these other New Testament occurrences of *Son of David*. Pay attention to the speaker, the audience, and the general context. Record your observations below.

John 7:37-52

Acts 2

Acts 13:22-41

Acts 15:14-21

Revelation 3:7; 5:5; 22:16

@THE END OF THE DAY . . .

As we close out our week of study, I hope you'll read the following Scriptures that summarize the Gospel in the Old Testament. Showing the Gospel this way is often referred to as "the Jerusalem Road," a pathway to help Jewish people who are still waiting for the Messiah.

All people are SINNERS.

Jeremiah 17:9

9 *The heart is more deceitful than all else and is desperately sick; who can understand it?*

Isaiah 64:6

6 *For all of us have become like one who is unclean, and all our righteous deeds are like a filthy garment; and all of us wither like a leaf, and our iniquities, like the wind, take us away.*

Isaiah 59:1-2

1 *Behold, the LORD's hand is not so short that it cannot save; nor is His ear so dull that it cannot hear.*

2 *But your iniquities have made a separation between you and your God, and your sins have hidden His face from you so that He does not hear.*

Sin brings God's judgment and DEATH.

Ezekiel 18:20

20 *The person who sins will die. The son will not bear the punishment for the father's iniquity, nor will the father bear the punishment for the son's iniquity; the righteousness of the righteous will be upon himself, and the wickedness of the wicked will be upon himself.*

God provides FORGIVENESS through blood sacrifice. Foreshadowed by the sacrificial system, the perfect blood of Messiah atones for the sins of man.

Leviticus 17:11

11 *'For the life of the flesh is in the blood, and I have given it to you on the altar to make atonement for your souls; for it is the blood by reason of the life that makes atonement.'*

Isaiah 53

1 *Who has believed our message? And to whom has the arm of the LORD been revealed?*

2 *For He grew up before Him like a tender shoot, and like a root out of parched ground; He has no stately form or majesty that we should look upon Him, nor appearance that we should be attracted to Him.*

3 *He was despised and forsaken of men, a man of sorrows and acquainted with grief; and like one from whom men hide their face He was despised, and we did not esteem Him.*

4 *Surely our griefs He Himself bore, and our sorrows He carried; yet we ourselves esteemed Him stricken, smitten of God, and afflicted.*

JESUS
SWEETEST NAME I KNOW

WHO JESUS IS AND WHY IT MATTERS

An Inductive Study of Christology

5   But He was pierced through for our transgressions, He was crushed for our iniquities; the chastening for our well-being fell upon Him, and by His scourging we are healed.

6   All of us like sheep have gone astray, each of us has turned to his own way; but the LORD has caused the iniquity of us all to fall on Him.

7   He was oppressed and He was afflicted, yet He did not open His mouth; like a lamb that is led to slaughter, and like a sheep that is silent before its shearers, so He did not open His mouth.

8   By oppression and judgment He was taken away; and as for His generation, who considered that He was cut off out of the land of the living for the transgression of my people, to whom the stroke was due?

9   His grave was assigned with wicked men, yet He was with a rich man in His death, because He had done no violence, nor was there any deceit in His mouth.

10 But the LORD was pleased to crush Him, putting Him to grief; if He would render Himself as a guilt offering, He will see His offspring, He will prolong His days, and the good pleasure of the LORD will prosper in His hand.

11 As a result of the anguish of His soul, He will see it and be satisfied; by His knowledge the Righteous One, My Servant, will justify the many, as He will bear their iniquities.

12 Therefore, I will allot Him a portion with the great, and He will divide the booty with the strong; because He poured out Himself to death, and was numbered with the transgressors; yet He Himself bore the sin of many, and interceded for the transgressors.

LIFE and SALVATION come through faith in God's Messiah.

Daniel 12:2

2   Many of those who sleep in the dust of the ground will awake, these to everlasting life, but the others to disgrace and everlasting contempt.

Genesis 15:6

6   Then he [Abram] believed in the LORD; and He reckoned it to him as righteousness.

Joel 2:32

32 "And it will come about that whoever calls on the name of the LORD
    Will be delivered;
    For on Mount Zion and in Jerusalem
    There will be those who escape,
    As the LORD has said,
    Even among the survivors whom the LORD calls."

Psalm 2:11-12

11 Worship the LORD with reverence
     And rejoice with trembling.

12 Do homage to the Son, that He not become angry, and you perish in the way,
     For His wrath may soon be kindled.
     How blessed are all who take refuge in Him!

Isaiah 55:1-6

1 "Ho! Every one who thirsts, come to the waters;
    And you who have no money come, buy and eat.
    Come, buy wine and milk
    Without money and without cost.

2 "Why do you spend money for what is not bread,
    And your wages for what does not satisfy?
    Listen carefully to Me, and eat what is good,
    And delight yourself in abundance.

3 "Incline your ear and come to Me.
    Listen, that you may live;
    And I will make an everlasting covenant with you,
    According to the faithful mercies shown to David.

4 "Behold, I have made him a witness to the peoples,
    A leader and commander for the peoples.

5 "Behold, you will call a nation you do not know,
    And a nation which knows you not will run to you,
    Because of the LORD your God, even the Holy One of Israel;
    For He has glorified you."

6 Seek the LORD while He may be found;
    Call upon Him while He is near.

JESUS
SWEETEST NAME I KNOW

WHO JESUS IS AND WHY IT MATTERS

An Inductive Study of Christology

Is Jesus "God"?

". . . before Abraham was born, I AM."
—Jesus, John 8:58

With final formulations of the Trinity and Incarnation at the Council of Chalcedon in AD 451, the Church officially began to speak of Christ as "fully God" and "fully man." But have you seen this in Scripture for yourself?

This week we'll examine Scriptures that relate to the "fully God" side.

FYI:

Why John Wrote His Gospel
"Therefore many other signs Jesus also performed in the presence of the disciples, which are not written in this book; but these have been written so that you may believe that Jesus is the Christ, the Son of God; and that believing you may have life in His name."

—John 20:30-31

ONE STEP FURTHER:

Marking a "Deity Chain" in Your Bible

In the margin by John 1:1 write **Deity: John 1:14.** This will direct you to the next verse in the chain. Repeat this process through list below.

When you arrive at Revelation 1:7-8, 17-18, in the margin write **Deity: John 1:1** which will complete the chain and bring you back to the beginning. The beauty in this is even if you can't remember where the chain starts, you can pick it up and follow it from any point you see the markings in your margins.

Here is the list you'll want to mark:

John 1:1

John 1:14

John 8:58-59

Exodus 3:14-15

John 8:24

John 10:30-33

Hebrews 1:3-4

Colossians 2:9-12

Colossians 1:15-20

John 20:27-29

John 17:5

Isaiah 42:8

Isaiah 7:14

Matthew 1:21-23

Isaiah 9:6

Isaiah 43:10-11

Micah 5:2

Luke 2:4-7, 10-11

Isaiah 44:6

Revelation 1:7-8, 17-18

Where we are . . .

This week we'll take a little different approach to our lesson, an approach that will yield an everyday tool you can keep in your Bible and use easily in a moment's notice. We are going to start in John 1:1 and trace references to the deity of Jesus Christ throughout the Bible.

What makes this exercise so powerful is that each reference leads to the next so you'll be able to talk a person through the biblical evidence for the deity of Christ right from your own Bible.

If you've taken *Precept Upon Precept*® courses before, you may have gone through this exercise. If you already have the references marked in your Bible you'll have a headstart, but we're going to take the references and go a little further this week.

OBSERVE the TEXT of SCRIPTURE

Our format will be different this week as we move through the deity chain grouping related texts.

JOHN: THE WORD "WAS WITH GOD AND WAS GOD"

While Matthew, writing to a heavily Jewish audience, focuses on Jesus as the Messiah, the prophesied Son of David, John focuses on Jesus as the Son of God. Because of this, John's Gospel will be most prominent this week as we query the deity of Jesus Christ.

READ the following verses from John's Gospel. As you do, **CIRCLE** every reference to *the Word* including pronouns and anything else the Word is said to be.

John 1:1, 14

1   In the beginning was the Word, and the Word was with God, and the Word was God.

14   And the Word became flesh, and dwelt among us, and we saw His glory, glory as of the only begotten from the Father, full of grace and truth.

DISCUSS with your GROUP or PONDER on your own . . .

How long has the Word existed?

JESUS
SWEETEST NAME I KNOW

WHO JESUS IS AND WHY IT MATTERS

An Inductive Study of Christology

What do we learn about the Word from John 1:1?

What did the Word do according to John 1:14? Does this help us identify and further define the Word? How?

How would you describe the Word to someone else? What elements are important and why?

JESUS: "BEFORE ABRAHAM WAS BORN, I AM"

What about Jesus Himself? Did He claim to be God? Let's look for answers in His own words.

READ the following verses from John and Exodus and **CIRCLE** every occurrence of the phrase *I am.*

John 8:58-59 [John 8, 9, and 10 take place in Jerusalem]

58 *Jesus said to them [the Jews], "Truly, truly, I say to you, before Abraham was born, I am."*

59 *Therefore they picked up stones to throw at Him, but Jesus hid Himself and went out of the temple.*

Exodus 3:14-15 [Moses has just asked God what His name is . . .]

14 *God said to Moses, "I AM WHO I AM"; and He said, "Thus you shall say to the sons of Israel, 'I AM has sent me to you.' "*

15 *God, furthermore, said to Moses, "Thus you shall say to the sons of Israel, 'The LORD, the God of your fathers, the God of Abraham, the God of Isaac, and the God of Jacob, has sent me to you.' This is My name forever, and this is My memorial-name to all generations.*

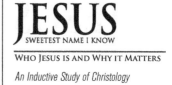

JESUS
SWEETEST NAME I KNOW

WHO JESUS IS AND WHY IT MATTERS

An Inductive Study of Christology

Week Four: **Is Jesus "God"?**

READ the following verses from John and **CIRCLE** every reference to *Jesus*, including synonyms and pronouns. Jesus is the initial speaker in both texts.

John 8:24 (cross-reference Deuteronomy 32:39 and Isaiah 43:10)

24 "Therefore I said to you that you will die in your sins; for unless you believe that I am He, you will die in your sins."

[Note: "He" is not in the original text.]

John 10:30-38

30 "I and the Father are one."

31 The Jews picked up stones again to stone Him.

32 Jesus answered them, "I showed you many good works from the Father; for which of them are you stoning Me?"

33 The Jews answered Him, "For a good work we do not stone You, but for blasphemy; and because You, being a man, make Yourself out to be God."

34 Jesus answered them, "Has it not been written in your Law, 'I SAID, YOU ARE GODS'?

35 "If he called them gods, to whom the word of God came (and the Scripture cannot be broken),

36 do you say of Him, whom the Father sanctified and sent into the world, 'You are blaspheming,' because I said, 'I am the Son of God'?

37 "If I do not do the works of My Father, do not believe Me;

38 but if I do them, though you do not believe Me, believe the works, so that you may know and understand that the Father is in Me, and I in the Father."

DISCUSS with your GROUP or PONDER on your own . . .

What did you learn from marking "I am" in John 8:58-59 and Exodus 3:14-15?

In John 8:58-59, what statement does Jesus make that so angers the Jews?

How does Jesus respond in verses 34-38?

What did Jesus say in John 8:24?

What does Jesus say in John 10:30-33 about His relationship to the Father?

Based on these passages, what claim do you think Jesus was making?

Considering the words and reactions of the Jewish people, what do you think they understood Him to be saying?

How do people react to the name of Jesus today when people claim He is God?

How should we present Jesus to others? Explain.

Do people who claim to know Jesus hedge on this? Is this a problem? Why?

ONE STEP FURTHER:

John 8 and Exodus 3

If you have extra time this week, read both John 8 and Exodus 3 to get the context for the verses we're looking at. Record your observations below.

John 8

Exodus 3

JESUS
SWEETEST NAME I KNOW

WHO JESUS IS AND WHY IT MATTERS

An Inductive Study of Christology

Digging Deeper

John: That You May Know that Jesus is the Christ, the Son of God

John tells us that his purpose in writing his Gospel is that people may know that Jesus is the Christ (i.e., the Messiah), the Son of God. If you have extra time this week, start reading through John's Gospel keeping his stated purpose in mind and note what you observe. Here are a few categories to get you going.

What miracles does John record to show Jesus' authority?

What "I am" statements does John record that tell us more about Jesus?

Based on your observations (and commentator's input after you've studied!), how does John's Gospel differ from the Synoptic Gospels? How is it similar?

What was your most significant takeaway from the Gospel of John?

PAUL AND THE AUTHOR OF HEBREWS: THE IMAGE OF THE INVISIBLE GOD AND EXACT REPRESENTATION OF HIS NATURE

While all Scripture is inspired by God, God used human beings in the process. The way John presents Jesus is distinctive to him. Same for Paul but both authors are consistent with the rest of the biblical account. Other voices include Jesus Himself, the prophet Isaiah, and the author of Hebrews.

READ the following verses from Hebrews and Colossians. As you read, **CIRCLE** every reference to *Jesus* including pronouns and synonyms and **UNDERLINE** every word or phrase that describes Him.

Hebrews 1:1-4

1 *God, after He spoke long ago to the fathers in the prophets in many portions and in many ways,*

2 *in these last days has spoken to us in His Son, whom He appointed heir of all things, through whom also He made the world.*

3 *And He is the radiance of His glory and the exact representation of His nature, and upholds all things by the word of His power. When He had made purification of sins, He sat down at the right hand of the Majesty on high,*

4 *having become as much better than the angels, as He has inherited a more excellent name than they.*

Colossians 2:9-12

9 *For in Him all the fullness of Deity dwells in bodily form,*

10 *and in Him you have been made complete, and He is the head over all rule and authority;*

11 *and in Him you were also circumcised with a circumcision made without hands, in the removal of the body of the flesh by the circumcision of Christ;*

12 *having been buried with Him in baptism, in which you were also raised up with Him through faith in the working of God, who raised Him from the dead.*

Colossians 1:15-20

15 *He is the image of the invisible God, the firstborn of all creation.*

16 *For by Him all things were created, both in the heavens and on earth, visible and invisible, whether thrones or dominions or rulers or authorities—all things have been created through Him and for Him.*

17 *He is before all things, and in Him all things hold together.*

18 *He is also head of the body, the church; and He is the beginning, the firstborn from the dead, so that He Himself will come to have first place in everything.*

19 *For it was the Father's good pleasure for all the fullness to dwell in Him,*

20 *and through Him to reconcile all things to Himself, having made peace through the blood of His cross; through Him, I say, whether things on earth or things in heaven.*

JESUS
SWEETEST NAME I KNOW
WHO JESUS IS AND WHY IT MATTERS
An Inductive Study of Christology

ONE STEP FURTHER:

Word Study: Exact Representation

What does the author of Hebrews mean when he says Jesus is the *exact representation* of God's nature? What two Greek terms are used and what do they mean? Record what you learn below.

Week Four: **Is Jesus "God"?**

DISCUSS with your GROUP or PONDER on your own . . .

How does the author of Hebrews describe Jesus in Hebrews 1:3-4?

Is Jesus distinct from God the Father? Is He different in nature? Explain from the text.

What does Jesus do? What has Jesus done?

How does Paul describe Jesus in the passages from Colossians?

What does Paul say about God the Father and how Jesus relates to Him?

Again, what does Jesus do? What has Jesus done?

How does this relate to you and me?

THOMAS: MY LORD AND MY GOD . . . THE GLORY OF THE FATHER

Support for Jesus' deity emerges in different ways. Sometimes Jesus declares a truth about Himself while other times He affirms those who finally figure it out. At still other times He makes statements that point to His deity. Let's take a look at some of these "ways" in several texts.

READ the following verses from John and Isaiah. Mark every reference to *God* with a **TRIANGLE.** Then **UNDERLINE** every form of the word *glory*.

John 20:27-29

[Jesus appears to Thomas after being resurrected from the dead.]

27 Then He said to Thomas, "Reach here with your finger, and see My hands; and reach here your hand and put it into My side; and do not be unbelieving, but believing."

28 Thomas answered and said to Him, "My Lord and my God!"

29 Jesus said to him, "Because you have seen Me, have you believed? Blessed are they who did not see, and yet believed."

John 17:5

5 "Now, Father, glorify Me together with Yourself, with the glory which I had with You before the world was.

Isaiah 42:8

8 "I am the LORD, that is My name; I will not give My glory to another, nor My praise to graven images.

JESUS
SWEETEST NAME I KNOW

WHO JESUS IS AND WHY IT MATTERS

An Inductive Study of Christology

Week Four: **Is Jesus "God"?**

DISCUSS with your GROUP or PONDER on your own . . .

What does Thomas say to Jesus in John 20:28?

What did Thomas need to believe?

How does the evidence he had compare to the evidence we have? Think through this carefully before you respond.

What does Jesus pray for in John 17:5? Why is He entitled to this?

What does Isaiah 42:8 say about God's willingness to share His glory?

How would you reconcile this with John 17:22?

Given this, what does this imply about Jesus in John 17?

Digging Deeper

Jesus and the Woman at the Well

If you have some extra time this week, read the account of Jesus and the woman at the well in John 4:1-43. This is the first time in the book of John where Jesus specifically tells someone that He is the Messiah.

Here are a few questions to get you going:

Who initiates the conversation at the well?

What social rules are being broken?

How does Jesus direct the conversation?

What does He tell the woman He has?

How does He demonstrate His power to her? Does this differ from the way He demonstrated it to others? If so, how?

According to Jesus, what kind of worshipers does the Father seek?

In verse 25, who does the woman say she knows is coming?

What does Jesus clearly reveal to her in verse 26?

How does the woman respond? How does the city respond?

What do they conclude about Jesus and why? How does this compare with the way people make decisions about Jesus today?

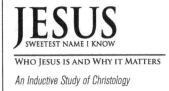

JESUS
SWEETEST NAME I KNOW

WHO JESUS IS AND WHY IT MATTERS

An Inductive Study of Christology

Week Four: **Is Jesus "God"?**

ISAIAH AND MATTHEW: THE SIGN OF A VIRGIN

Although we've looked at a number of these verses, they are important to review in our present context.

READ the following verses and mark every reference to *God* (include pronouns and synonyms) with a **TRIANGLE. CIRCLE** every reference to *Jesus*. **UNDERLINE** every form of the word *save* or *savior*.

Isaiah 7:14

14 "Therefore the Lord Himself will give you a sign: Behold, a virgin will be with child and bear a son, and she will call His name Immanuel."

Matthew 1:21-23

21 "She will bear a Son; and you shall call His name Jesus, for He will save His people from their sins."

22 Now all this took place to fulfill what was spoken by the Lord through the prophet:

23 "BEHOLD, THE VIRGIN SHALL BE WITH CHILD AND SHALL BEAR A SON, AND THEY SHALL CALL HIS NAME IMMANUEL," which translated means, "GOD WITH US."

Isaiah 9:6

6 For a child will be born to us, a son will be given to us; and the government will rest on His shoulders; and His name will be called Wonderful Counselor, Mighty God, Eternal Father, Prince of Peace.

Isaiah 43:10-11

10 "You are My witnesses," declares the LORD, "And My servant whom I have chosen, so that you may know and believe Me and understand that I am He. Before Me there was no God formed, and there will be none after Me.

11 "I, even I, am the LORD, and there is no savior besides Me."

DISCUSS with your GROUP or PONDER on your own . . .

What does the Lord promise in Isaiah 7:14?

Who is born according to Matthew 1:21-23? What is He going to do for His people?

What does His name mean?

According to Isaiah 9:6, what will this son be called?

According to Isaiah 43:10-11, who is the only Savior?

Taken together, what do these verses say about the Son born of the virgin? Who is He?

How is God characterized throughout these verses? What confidence does this give you for living?

Digging Deeper

Colossians

Paul begins his letter to the church at Colossae by emphasizing who Christ is and explaining why it matters. This emphasis on the person and work of Jesus may have been due to a shift away from the truth or a reaction to local Jewish speculation on ranks of angels which was rampant. If you have some time this week, read the entire book of Colossians and record everything you learn about Jesus. Here are a couple of major categories to help frame your thinking.

What does Paul tell us about Jesus?

Why do these things matter? What errors do you think Paul was correcting?

Do we need to correct false teaching about Jesus today? What and how?

ONE STEP FURTHER:

Memorize It!

If you're inclined toward memorizing Scripture, think about investing some time in hiding in your heart key Christological passages or books. Here are a few to consider:

Isaiah 53

John 1:1-18

Philippians 2:1-11

The Epistle to the Colossians

The Epistle to the Hebrews

Revelation 1

MICAH: THE SIGN OF BETHLEHEM

Since we've already gone over Micah's prophesy, we'll review this portion briefly.

READ the following verses and **CIRCLE** every reference to Jesus. **UNDERLINE** titles that apply to Him.

Micah 5:2

2 *"But as for you, Bethlehem Ephrathah, too little to be among the clans of Judah, from you One will go forth for Me to be ruler in Israel. His goings forth are from long ago, from the days of eternity."*

Luke 2:4-7, 10-11

4 *Joseph also went up from Galilee, from the city of Nazareth, to Judea, to the city of David which is called Bethlehem, because he was of the house and family of David,*

5 *in order to register along with Mary, who was engaged to him, and was with child.*

6 *While they were there, the days were completed for her to give birth.*

7 *And she gave birth to her firstborn son; and she wrapped Him in cloths, and laid Him in a manger, because there was no room for them in the inn.*

10 *But the angel said to them, "Do not be afraid; for behold, I bring you good news of great joy which will be for all the people;*

11 *for today in the city of David there has been born for you a Savior, who is Christ the Lord."*

DISCUSS with your GROUP or PONDER on your own . . .

Where will the ruler of Israel come from?

How far back are His "goings forth"?

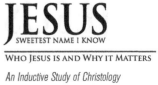

Week Four: **Is Jesus "God"?**

What is the Child called in Luke 2:11?

ONE STEP FURTHER:

Isaiah 44 and Revelation 1
If you have extra time this week, read these two chapters. Record your observations below. Pay attention to who is speaking, who the audience is, and what you learn about God.

Isaiah 44

Revelation 1

Again, who is the only Savior according to Isaiah 43:11?

Therefore, who is this Child?

ISAIAH AND JESUS: GOD THE FIRST AND THE LAST

Our final two passages tie together God's words through the prophets Isaiah and John.

READ the following verses and **BOX** each phrase that begins with an "I am."

Isaiah 44:6

6 *"Thus says the LORD, the King of Israel and his Redeemer, the LORD of hosts: 'I am the first and I am the last, and there is no God besides Me.'"*

Revelation 1:7-8, 17-18

7 *BEHOLD, HE IS COMING WITH THE CLOUDS, and every eye will see Him, even those who pierced Him; and all the tribes of the earth will mourn over Him. So it is to be. Amen.*

8 *"I am the Alpha and the Omega," says the Lord God, "who is and who was and who is to come, the Almighty."*

17 *When I saw Him, I fell at His feet like a dead man. And He placed His right hand on me, saying, "Do not be afraid; I am the first and the last,*

18 *and the living One; and I was dead, and behold, I am alive forevermore, and I have the keys of death and of Hades."*

DISCUSS with your GROUP or PONDER on your own . . .

What does the LORD say about Himself in Isaiah 44:6? List everything He says He is.

Who does Revelation 1:7 describe? Explain your reasoning.

Who does Revelation 1:8 refer to? Explain your reasoning.

Who is described in Revelation 1:17-18? Again, explain your reasoning.

Who is "the first and the last"? What significance does this have for you today?

WHO JESUS IS AND WHY IT MATTERS

An Inductive Study of Christology

@THE END OF THE DAY . . .

Take some time to think through all of the truths about Jesus that you've learned and reviewed this week. You might want to page back through what we've studied or simply jot down below what God brings to mind. Then, looking back at these truths, pray and ask God to help you apply these truths about Jesus to the situations you find yourself in this week.

Is Jesus "Man"?

*For there is one God, and one mediator also between
God and men, the man Christ Jesus . . .*
−1 Timothy 2:5

Over the past several weeks we've looked at Jesus Christ from a number of different perspectives that have cut across the pages of Scripture. We've looked at His pre-existence, His fulfillment of the Son of David prophecy, and the thorough witness of the Bible to Him as the Son of God. This week we'll examine more closely some key passages in the Bible that tell us about the humanity of Jesus Christ.

Week Five: **Is Jesus "Man"?**

OBSERVE the TEXT of SCRIPTURE

As we start off this week in the short book of Philippians, we're going to look carefully at context as we approach the text inductively.

READ the four-chapter book of Philippians and answer the following questions:

Who wrote it? What does the text tell us about the author?

Who was it written to? What do we know about the recipients from the text?

What type of literature is Philippians?

What are some key words and phrases?

What is the overall theme of the book?

When was Philippians written?

Where was it written from?

Why did the author write the letter?

Having considered the context, let's look more closely at the Christological section in Philippians 2.

READ Philippians 2. **CIRCLE** every reference to *Jesus*. Put a **TRIANGLE** over every reference to *God the Father*.

Philippians 2:5-11

5   Have this attitude in yourselves which was also in Christ Jesus,

6   who, although He existed in the form of God, did not regard equality with God a thing to be grasped,

7   but emptied Himself, taking the form of a bond-servant, and being made in the likeness of men.

8   Being found in appearance as a man, He humbled Himself by becoming obedient to the point of death, even death on a cross.

9   For this reason also, God highly exalted Him, and bestowed on Him the name which is above every name,

10 so that at the name of Jesus EVERY KNEE WILL BOW, of those who are in heaven and on earth and under the earth,

11 and that every tongue will confess that Jesus Christ is Lord, to the glory of God the Father.

DISCUSS with your GROUP or PONDER on your own . . .

What are your initial observations on the text?

ONE STEP FURTHER:

Word Study: Attitude
If you have some extra time this week, see if you can find the Greek word translated "attitude." Where else does it appear in this chapter, in this book, in the rest of Paul's writings and in the New Testament at large? Record your observations below.

WHO JESUS IS AND WHY IT MATTERS

An Inductive Study of Christology

88

Notes

Describe Jesus from the text. Who is He? What did He do? How will people eventually respond to Him?

What does the text teach about God?

Describe the relationship between Christ and God.

What qualities characterize Jesus particularly with regard to His relationship to God?

What did God do to Jesus?

JESUS
SWEETEST NAME I KNOW

WHO JESUS IS AND WHY IT MATTERS

An Inductive Study of Christology

Week Five: **Is Jesus "Man"?**

In the end, how will people regard Jesus? Will there be any exceptions? Where do you see this in the text?

Are any words in this section unclear to you? If so, which ones? Why?

How can you investigate them?

What rubber-meets-the-road application does Paul take from these truths about the person and work of Jesus?

How does Jesus' example help us think more accurately about ourselves? How should it affect our behavior?

How can you specifically apply what you've learned from the text this week?

Digging Deeper

Exploring the Kenosis Passage

Philippians 2 is sometimes referred to as the Kenosis Passage, taken from the Greek verb *kenoo* (empty) used in 2:7. If you have some extra time this week and feel up to it, see what you can discover by studying the Greek roots behind the following English words:

Form (vv. 6, 7)

Equality (v. 6)

Grasped (v. 6)

Likeness (v. 7)

Appearance (v. 8)

Emptied (v. 7)

Lord (v. 11)

JESUS
SWEETEST NAME I KNOW

WHO JESUS IS AND WHY IT MATTERS

An Inductive Study of Christology

OBSERVE the TEXT of SCRIPTURE

READ Hebrews 1. **CIRCLE** every reference to *Jesus*. Put a **TRIANGLE** over every reference to *God* including synonyms and pronouns. Be sure to mark pronouns so you know which subject (antecedent) each one refers to.

Hebrews 1

1   *God, after He spoke long ago to the fathers in the prophets in many portions and in many ways,*

2   *in these last days has spoken to us in His Son, whom He appointed heir of all things, through whom also He made the world.*

3   *And He is the radiance of His glory and the exact representation of His nature, and upholds all things by the word of His power. When He had made purification of sins, He sat down at the right hand of the Majesty on high,*

4   *having become as much better than the angels, as He has inherited a more excellent name than they.*

5   *For to which of the angels did He ever say, "YOU ARE MY SON, TODAY I HAVE BEGOTTEN YOU"? And again, "I WILL BE A FATHER TO HIM AND HE SHALL BE A SON TO ME"?*

6   *And when He again brings the firstborn into the world, He says, "AND LET ALL THE ANGELS OF GOD WORSHIP HIM."*

7   *And of the angels He says, "WHO MAKES HIS ANGELS WINDS, AND HIS MINISTERS A FLAME OF FIRE."*

8   *But of the Son He says, "YOUR THRONE, O GOD, IS FOREVER AND EVER, AND THE RIGHTEOUS SCEPTER IS THE SCEPTER OF HIS KINGDOM.*

9   *"YOU HAVE LOVED RIGHTEOUSNESS AND HATED LAWLESSNESS; THEREFORE GOD, YOUR GOD, HAS ANOINTED YOU WITH THE OIL OF GLADNESS ABOVE YOUR COMPANIONS."*

10 *And, "YOU, LORD, IN THE BEGINNING LAID THE FOUNDATION OF THE EARTH, AND THE HEAVENS ARE THE WORKS OF YOUR HANDS;*

11 *THEY WILL PERISH, BUT YOU REMAIN; AND THEY ALL WILL BECOME OLD LIKE A GARMENT,*

12 *AND LIKE A MANTLE YOU WILL ROLL THEM UP; LIKE A GARMENT THEY WILL ALSO BE CHANGED. BUT YOU ARE THE SAME, AND YOUR YEARS WILL NOT COME TO AN END."*

13 *But to which of the angels has He ever said, "SIT AT MY RIGHT HAND, UNTIL I MAKE YOUR ENEMIES A FOOTSTOOL FOR YOUR FEET"?*

14 *Are they not all ministering spirits, sent out to render service for the sake of those who will inherit salvation?*

JESUS
SWEETEST NAME I KNOW

WHO JESUS IS AND WHY IT MATTERS

An Inductive Study of Christology

DISCUSS with your GROUP or PONDER on your own . . .

How has God's communication with people changed over time?

FYI:

Fellow Heirs with Christ
The Spirit Himself testifies with our spirit that we are children of God, and if children, heirs also, heirs of God and fellow heirs with Christ, if indeed we suffer with Him so that we may also be glorified with Him.

—Romans 8:16-17

What facts do we learn about Jesus in Hebrews 1:2?

How does the author of Hebrews describe the relationship between Jesus and God in Hebrews 1:3? (The **ONE STEP FURTHER** section will help you with the word pictures.)

According to Hebrews 1:8, what does God say "of the Son"?

What other words describe Jesus in this chapter?

What characteristics are attributed to the Son?

JESUS
SWEETEST NAME I KNOW

WHO JESUS IS AND WHY IT MATTERS

An Inductive Study of Christology

Notes

Digging Deeper

Hebrews 1 Quotations

The author of Hebrews digs into the Psaltar for significant chapter-one material. If you have time this week, read through the Psalms and record what you discover about the original context of each verse or set of verses he quotes.

Psalm 2

Psalm 45

Psalm 102

Psalm 104

Psalm 110

ONE STEP FURTHER:

These Last Days

The author of Hebrews tells his readers that "in these last days" God has spoken to us literally "in [or 'by'] son." The term "last days" *(eschatos ho hemera)* refers to the time period between Jesus' first and second comings. If you have extra time this week, compare Jesus' uses of the singluar "the last day" and the plural "the last days" elsewhere in the New Testament. Note what characterizes the last days and record your findings below.

JESUS
SWEETEST NAME I KNOW
WHO JESUS IS AND WHY IT MATTERS
An Inductive Study of Christology

What did the Son "become" relative to the angels according to Hebrews 1:4?

Based on what you know of the Gospels, what has God "spoken to us in His Son" in these last days?

What does Hebrews 1 say about the Son's past?

What does it teach about the Son's future?

According to Hebrews 2:1, why is it so critical that we listen to Jesus?

How well do you think our culture listens?

Can you improve your listening? If so, how?

Notes

ONE STEP FURTHER:

How did they hear?

If you have some extra time this week, compare the ways God spoke prior to His Son with how He spoke through Him according to Hebrews 1 and 2. Record your findings below.

JESUS
SWEETEST NAME I KNOW

WHO JESUS IS AND WHY IT MATTERS

An Inductive Study of Christology

Digging Deeper

Isaiah's Servant Songs

Isaiah 42:1-4, 49:1-6, 50:4-11, and 52:13–53:1-12 are distinctly referred to as Servant Songs. If you have extra time this week, examine the first three Songs for yourself to see what Isaiah says about the Servant of the Lord. We'll look at Isaiah 52:13–53:1-12 in the main portion of the study.

OBSERVE the TEXT of SCRIPTURE

READ the Servant Songs from Isaiah. In each, **CIRCLE** every reference to the *Servant* and **UNDERLINE** every descriptive phrase referring to the Servant. After each Song, you'll be prompted to create a list of what you've learned based on your markings.

Isaiah 42:1-4

1 *"Behold, My Servant, whom I uphold; My chosen one in whom My soul delights. I have put My Spirit upon Him; He will bring forth justice to the nations.*

2 *"He will not cry out or raise His voice, nor make His voice heard in the street.*

3 *"A bruised reed He will not break and a dimly burning wick He will not extinguish; He will faithfully bring forth justice.*

4 *"He will not be disheartened or crushed until He has established justice in the earth; and the coastlands will wait expectantly for His law."*

The Servant in Isaiah 42:1-4

What He Is / Will Do	What He Will NOT Do
He is God's Servant (v. 1)	He will not cry out (v. 2)

Isaiah 49:1-6

1 Listen to Me, O islands, and pay attention, you peoples from afar. The LORD called Me from the womb; from the body of My mother He named Me.

2 He has made My mouth like a sharp sword, in the shadow of His hand He has concealed Me; and He has also made Me a select arrow, He has hidden Me in His quiver.

3 He said to Me, "You are My Servant, Israel, in Whom I will show My glory."

4 But I said, "I have toiled in vain, I have spent My strength for nothing and vanity; yet surely the justice due to Me is with the LORD, and My reward with My God."

5 And now says the LORD, who formed Me from the womb to be His Servant, to bring Jacob back to Him, so that Israel might be gathered to Him (for I am honored in the sight of the LORD, and My God is My strength),

6 He says, "It is too small a thing that You should be My Servant to raise up the tribes of Jacob and to restore the preserved ones of Israel; I will also make You a light of the nations so that My salvation may reach to the end of the earth."

The Servant in Isaiah 49:1-6

What He Is / Will Do

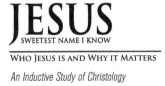

Week Five: **Is Jesus "Man"?**

Isaiah 50:4-11

4 The Lord GOD has given Me the tongue of disciples, that I may know how to sustain the weary one with a word. He awakens Me morning by morning, He awakens My ear to listen as a disciple.

5 The Lord GOD has opened My ear; and I was not disobedient nor did I turn back.

6 I gave My back to those who strike Me, and My cheeks to those who pluck out the beard; I did not cover My face from humiliation and spitting.

7 For the Lord GOD helps Me, therefore, I am not disgraced; therefore, I have set My face like flint, and I know that I will not be ashamed.

8 He who vindicates Me is near; who will contend with Me? Let us stand up to each other; who has a case against Me? Let him draw near to Me.

9 Behold, the Lord GOD helps Me; who is he who condemns Me? Behold, they will all wear out like a garment; the moth will eat them.

10 Who is among you that fears the LORD, that obeys the voice of His servant, that walks in darkness and has no light? Let him trust in the name of the LORD and rely on his God.

11 Behold, all you who kindle a fire, who encircle yourselves with firebrands, walk in the light of your fire and among the brands you have set ablaze. This you will have from My hand: you will lie down in torment.

The Servant in Isaiah 50:4-11

What He Is / Will Do	What He Will NOT Do

AN OVERVIEW OF THE TEXT

The most famous of the Servant Songs and the one most clearly pointing to the person of Jesus Christ is Isaiah 53. We'll look at this one together, picking up the final three verses of Isaiah 52.

OBSERVE the TEXT of SCRIPTURE

READ Isaiah 52:13-53:12. **CIRCLE** every reference to the *Servant* and **UNDERLINE** every descriptive phrase referring to the Servant.

Isaiah 52:13-15

13 Behold, My servant will prosper, He will be high and lifted up and greatly exalted.

14 Just as many were astonished at you, My people, so His appearance was marred more than any man and His form more than the sons of men.

15 Thus He will sprinkle many nations, kings will shut their mouths on account of Him; for what had not been told them they will see, and what they had not heard they will understand.

Isaiah 53:1-12

1 Who has believed our message? And to whom has the arm of the LORD been revealed?

2 For He grew up before Him like a tender shoot, and like a root out of parched ground; He has no stately form or majesty that we should look upon Him, nor appearance that we should be attracted to Him.

3 He was despised and forsaken of men, a man of sorrows and acquainted with grief; and like one from whom men hide their face He was despised, and we did not esteem Him.

4 Surely our griefs He Himself bore, and our sorrows He carried; yet we ourselves esteemed Him stricken, smitten of God, and afflicted.

5 But He was pierced through for our transgressions, He was crushed for our iniquities; the chastening for our well-being fell upon Him, and by His scourging we are healed.

6 All of us like sheep have gone astray, each of us has turned to his own way; but the LORD has caused the iniquity of us all to fall on Him.

7 He was oppressed and He was afflicted, yet He did not open His mouth; like a lamb that is led to slaughter, and like a sheep that is silent before its shearers, so He did not open His mouth.

8 By oppression and judgment He was taken away; and as for His generation, who considered that He was cut off out of the land of the living for the transgression of my people, to whom the stroke was due?

9 His grave was assigned with wicked men, yet He was with a rich man in His death, because He had done no violence, nor was there any deceit in His mouth.

JESUS
SWEETEST NAME I KNOW

WHO JESUS IS AND WHY IT MATTERS

An Inductive Study of Christology

10 *But the LORD was pleased to crush Him, putting Him to grief; if He would render Himself as a guilt offering, He will see His offspring, He will prolong His days, and the good pleasure of the LORD will prosper in His hand.*

11 *As a result of the anguish of His soul, He will see it and be satisfied; by His knowledge the Righteous One, My Servant, will justify the many, as He will bear their iniquities.*

12 *Therefore, I will allot Him a portion with the great, and He will divide the booty with the strong; because He poured out Himself to death, and was numbered with the transgressors; yet He Himself bore the sin of many, and interceded for the transgressors.*

DISCUSS with your GROUP or PONDER on your own . . .

Compare this Servant Song with the accounts of the Gospel writers and make a chart to show how they compare.

The Description of the Servant	The Person and Work of Jesus

The Description of the Servant	The Person and Work of Jesus

Does Isaiah's Servant of the Lord refer to the nation of Israel, Jesus, or both? Give reasons for your answer.

Week Five: **Is Jesus "Man"?**

Digging Deeper

A Personal Look at the Deity of Jesus

Knowing the biblical truth about Jesus Christ is critical. In a day and age where feelings rule, never forget that true faith is grounded in the fact of the Word of God. Still, we don't want to leave the facts on a shelf. True and healthy Christianity lives day-to-day in the personal reality of the facts of the Gospel as they are appropriated and lived out. So this week, if you have some extra time, list the attributes of Jesus you learned and then record how each one can affect your walk with Him.

Because Jesus is _____ , I . . .

Because Jesus is _____ , I . . .

Because Jesus is _____ , I . . .

Because Jesus is _____ , I . . .

Because Jesus is _____ , I . . .

Because Jesus is _____ , I . . .

Because Jesus is _____ , I . . .

Because Jesus is _____ , I . . .

Because Jesus is _____ , I . . .

Because Jesus is _____ , I . . .

@THE END OF THE DAY . . .

Take some time as we close our study this week to think back over all you've learned about Jesus so far in our time together. What is the most significant truth you've discovered? How has it impacted your life?

How would you explain the deity of Jesus Christ to a person knocking at your door who wants to tell you that Jesus is one of many gods?

The person, nature, and work of Jesus Christ are the heart of the Gospel—
God became flesh to save mankind. Jesus Christ, 100% God and 100% man,
is "the way, the truth, and life" (John 14:6). The only way to the Father is through
Him.

Is Jesus High Priest and King?

For we do not have a high priest who cannot sympathize with our weaknesses, but One who has been tempted in all things as we are, yet without sin.
–Hebrews 4:15

What Jesus *is* matters. It matters because Jesus Christ is the center of Christian faith. To be askew on the Second Coming, on baptism, or any one of scores of other biblical topics is akin to being down the street from the intended destination. To be wrong on who Jesus is . . . is to have navigated to the wrong country. Jesus is that big of a deal. Truth about Him divides true from false belief, hope from despair, right from wrong, heaven from hell.

But there is more. The incarnation of God not only gives us hope for eternity in His presence but also a very present help today. As we finish our study, we're going to look at the ramifications of the humanity of Jesus Christ–our Great High Priest who is "able to save forever those who draw near to God through Him" (Hebrews 7:25).

Week Six: **Is Jesus High Priest and King?**

REVIEW

Before we dive in today, take a little time to review what you've learned so far about Jesus Christ. I've provided a few broad categories below, but feel free to add any additional comments in the "Jesus is . . ." section.

Jesus before Christmas . . .

Jesus in the Old Testament . . .

Jesus as the Son of David . . .

Jesus is God incarnate . . .

Jesus is . . .

Questions I still have . . .

JESUS
SWEETEST NAME I KNOW

WHO JESUS IS AND WHY IT MATTERS

An Inductive Study of Christology

Where we are . . .

In the Gospel of John we saw that the Word became flesh and dwelt among us. Jesus took on the form of a bondservant becoming a man to save us. We've looked at aspects of Jesus' humanity as we've walked through our study thus far. Other things that Scripture tells us about Jesus we haven't looked at specifically, but as you read the Word you'll see for yourself that Jesus did the normal things human beings do: He was born and grew up, He got hungry and thirsty, He ate and drank, He got tired and slept. He experienced sorrow and grief and tears. He lived and He died.

Moreover, sin required a perfect sacrifice that only Jesus could provide. Jesus qualified to be not only the sacrifice for our sins but also our perfect High Priest who can sympathize and can come to our aid in time of need because he "lived out" our weak condition.

OBSERVE the TEXT of SCRIPTURE

In 1 Corinthians 15:1-8 Paul summarizes the work of Jesus Christ, the Gospel.

READ 1 Corinthians 15:1-8 and **CIRCLE** every reference to *Christ* (including pronouns). **UNDERLINE** everything He did.

1 Corinthians 15:1-8

1 *Now I make known to you, brethren, the gospel which I preached to you, which also you received, in which also you stand,*

2 *by which also you are saved, if you hold fast the word which I preached to you, unless you believed in vain.*

3 *For I delivered to you as of first importance what I also received, that Christ died for our sins according to the Scriptures,*

4 *and that He was buried, and that He was raised on the third day according to the Scriptures,*

5 *and that He appeared to Cephas, then to the twelve.*

6 *After that He appeared to more than five hundred brethren at one time, most of whom remain until now, but some have fallen asleep;*

7 *then He appeared to James, then to all the apostles;*

8 *and last of all, as to one untimely born, He appeared to me also.*

ONE STEP FURTHER:

According to the Scriptures

If you have extra time this week, read Psalm 22 and compare how the details of David's psalm match up with the life of Jesus Christ.

JESUS
SWEETEST NAME I KNOW

WHO JESUS IS AND WHY IT MATTERS

An Inductive Study of Christology

Notes

DISCUSS with your GROUP or PONDER on your own . . .

What does the Gospel do for those who believe?

FYI:

Gospel
"Gospel" is Greek for good news.

What message about Christ did Paul first receive and then deliver? What did Jesus do?

What "Scriptures" (v. 4) do you think Paul is referring to?

Do you think Paul's usage of "Christ" in this passage (as opposed to "Jesus") is significant? If so, explain why.

Did you notice any repeated words or phrases? If so, what are they and why are they significant?

How does Paul authenticate this Gospel he is talking about?

According to 1 Corinthians 15:1-8, what are the key elements of the Gospel message?

OBSERVE the TEXT of SCRIPTURE

Because of the resurrection of Jesus, we who believe in Him have the hope of resurrection one day (see **ONE STEP FURTHER**). But as good as the future promise is, we also have a present help, a High Priest who understands, who has worn flesh and blood, borne our sins, and paid the penalty for them.

READ Hebrews 4:14-16 and **CIRCLE** every reference to *Jesus*, our *great high priest*.

Hebrews 4:14-16 — (Because He is man . . . He can sympathize)

14 *Therefore, since we have a great high priest who has passed through the heavens, Jesus the Son of God, let us hold fast our confession.*

15 *For we do not have a high priest who cannot sympathize with our weaknesses, but One who has been tempted in all things as we are, yet without sin.*

16 *Therefore let us draw near with confidence to the throne of grace, so that we may receive mercy and find grace to help in time of need.*

DISCUSS with your GROUP or PONDER on your own . . .

How does the author of Hebrews refer to Jesus in this section?

Notes

ONE STEP FURTHER:

Romans 8:11 / 1 John 3:2
Our hope of resurrection is grounded in the resurrection of Jesus Christ Himself. If you have some extra time this week. Read Romans 8:11 and 1 John 3:2-3 taking note of the hope we have, why we have it, what we can expect in the future based on who we are in Christ, and how it actually changes us in this life. Record your findings below.

JESUS
SWEETEST NAME I KNOW

WHO JESUS IS AND WHY IT MATTERS
An Inductive Study of Christology

Week Six: **Is Jesus High Priest and King?**

What can our high priest do for us? Why?

How is His priesthood different from the Levites'?

Why can we draw near with confidence to the throne of grace? What will we find there?

Where do you typically go during times of need? Do you go to the throne of grace or elsewhere? Why?

OBSERVE the TEXT of SCRIPTURE

READ Hebrews 9:11-14 and 27-28. **CIRCLE** every reference to *Christ* including pronouns. Then **UNDERLINE** every occurrence of *blood*.

Hebrews 9:11-14, 27-28 — (Because He is not merely man . . . He can save!)

11 *But when Christ appeared as a high priest of the good things to come,* He entered *through the greater and more perfect tabernacle, not made with hands, that is to say, not of this creation;*

12 *and not through the blood of goats and calves, but through His own blood, He entered the holy place once for all, having obtained eternal redemption.*

13 *For if the blood of goats and bulls and the ashes of a heifer sprinkling those who have been defiled sanctify for the cleansing of the flesh,*

14 *how much more will the blood of Christ, who through the eternal Spirit offered Himself without blemish to God, cleanse your conscience from dead works to serve the living God?*

Hebrews 9:27-28

27 *And inasmuch as it is appointed for men to die once and after this comes judgment,*

28 *so Christ also, having been offered once to bear the sins of many, will appear a second time for salvation without reference to sin, to those who eagerly await Him.*

DISCUSS with your GROUP or PONDER on your own . . .

What does this tell us about Christ?

What is He called?

What major comparison does the author make in verses 11-14?

How is Jesus' blood better? What does it do?

According to verse 28, why did Jesus come to earth the first time? Why will He come the second time?

Do you live in the truth of verse 14? Explain.

JESUS
SWEETEST NAME I KNOW

WHO JESUS IS AND WHY IT MATTERS

An Inductive Study of Christology

Digging Deeper

First John and Docetism

FYI:

What is Docetism?

Making a sharp distinction between the physical and spiritual, Docetism claims Jesus was not truly human. The name comes from the Greek word *dokein*, "to seem." In denying the incarnation docetism also denies Jesus' suffering, death, and resurrection.

In 1 John, the apostle John argues diligently for Jesus' real (as opposed to apparent) humanity and the true knowledge Christians possess in Him. If you have some extra time this week, scour John's first letter and record your observations below. Here are a few questions to get you started.

How does John focus on the reality of the incarnation of Jesus Christ? What specifics does he present?

How does John use the words *know* and *knowledge?* How can people know they are in relationship with Jesus?

What does he say about deceivers? How do they differ from those who truly know Christ?

According to 1 John, how can we identify and differentiate the Spirit of God from the Spirit of Antichrist?

OBSERVE the TEXT of SCRIPTURE

Acts 1 tells us that Jesus ascended to heaven 40 days after His resurrection. This, however, is not the end of the story. The consistent witness of Scripture is that He is coming again.

READ 1 Thessalonians 4:13-18. **CIRCLE** every reference to *Jesus*. **UNDERLINE** every occurrence of *asleep*.

I Thessalonians 4:13-18

13 *But we do not want you to be uninformed, brethren, about those who are asleep, so that you will not grieve as do the rest who have no hope.*

14 *For if we believe that Jesus died and rose again, even so God will bring with Him those who have fallen asleep in Jesus.*

15 *For this we say to you by the word of the Lord, that we who are alive and remain until the coming of the Lord, will not precede those who have fallen asleep.*

16 *For the Lord Himself will descend from heaven with a shout, with the voice of the archangel and with the trumpet of God, and the dead in Christ will rise first.*

17 *Then we who are alive and remain will be caught up together with them in the clouds to meet the Lord in the air, and so we shall always be with the Lord.*

18 *Therefore comfort one another with these words.*

DISCUSS with your GROUP or PONDER on your own . . .

Paul talks about those who "have fallen asleep in Jesus." What is he referring to? Explain your reasoning.

Why do these people have hope?

FYI:

Gnosticism and Neo-Gnosticism

The term Gnosticism comes from the Greek word *gnosis* meaning knowledge. Like Docetic thinking, Gnosticism saw the world from a dualistic perspective: physical is evil and spiritual good. Beyond this, however, Gnosticism taught a "special knowledge" that made some people better or more spiritual than others.

Gnosticism rears its head from time to time. When you see dualism and/or "special knowledge" apart from the revealed truth of God's Word, be aware that you may be tangling with Gnostic thinking.

FYI:

A Gentle Reminder from Peter

Neo-Gnosticim appeals because secrets appeal and pride calls. God's Word is clear that we don't need hidden knowledge to live godly lives. God has given us everything we need:

Grace and peace be multiplied to you in the knowledge of God and of Jesus our Lord; seeing that His divine power has granted to us everything pertaining to life and godliness, through the true knowledge of Him who called us by His own glory and excellence.

—2 Peter 1:2-3

JESUS
SWEETEST NAME I KNOW

WHO JESUS IS AND WHY IT MATTERS

An Inductive Study of Christology

Week Six: **Is Jesus High Priest and King?**

What does Paul tell us here about Jesus? What has happened to Him? What will happen?

What hope does this give you today?

Who in your life needs this hope?

Do you live in the reality of this hope? If so, how does it change your outlook and behavior day to day? If not, how can you begin to live this truth more fully?

OBSERVE the TEXT of SCRIPTURE

READ Hebrews 13:8.

Hebrews 13:8

> 8 *Jesus Christ is the same yesterday and today and forever.*

DISCUSS with your GROUP or PONDER on your own . . .

What does this text tell us about how the Jesus of the Bible compares with the Jesus we will meet one day in heaven?

JESUS
SWEETEST NAME I KNOW
WHO JESUS IS AND WHY IT MATTERS
An Inductive Study of Christology

Digging Deeper

The I AM passages . . . what does Jesus claim?

The Gospel of John uniquely records Jesus defining Himself with a number of I AM statements. If you have some extra time this week, read through this book. Record these statements and see what you can discover about each.

Jesus said: "I am the . . ."

What?	Verse	Meaning?	Impact?
Door	10:9	Entry to the safety of a flock.	Jesus will protect me like a shepherd guards his sheep.

Week Six: **Is Jesus High Priest and King?**

OBSERVE the TEXT of SCRIPTURE

Will Jesus return to earth? Where is He now and how does He appear?

READ John's words about Jesus in Revelation 1:7 and 12-18. **UNDERLINE** every phrase that describes Jesus.

Revelation 1:7, 12-18

7 BEHOLD, HE IS COMING WITH THE CLOUDS, and every eye will see Him, even those who pierced Him; and all the tribes of the earth will mourn over Him. So it is to be. Amen.

12 Then I turned to see the voice that was speaking with me. And having turned I saw seven golden lampstands;

13 and in the middle of the lampstands I saw one like a son of man, clothed in a robe reaching to the feet, and girded across His chest with a golden sash.

14 His head and His hair were white like white wool, like snow; and His eyes were like a flame of fire.

15 His feet were like burnished bronze, when it has been made to glow in a furnace, and His voice was like the sound of many waters.

16 In His right hand He held seven stars, and out of His mouth came a sharp two-edged sword; and His face was like the sun shining in its strength.

17 When I saw Him, I fell at His feet like a dead man. And He placed His right hand on me, saying, "Do not be afraid; I am the first and the last,

18 and the living One; and I was dead, and behold, I am alive forevermore, and I have the keys of death and of Hades.

DISCUSS with your GROUP or PONDER on your own . . .

What, if anything, in this picture of Jesus is similar to what John knew of Him before His ascension?

How has His appearance changed?

ONE STEP FURTHER:

Daniel 7, Matthew 17 and Mark 9

If you have time this week, explore and compare the following accounts. I'll give you verse ranges but remember: it's always best to read entire chapters for context.

Daniel 7:9-15

Matthew 17:1-9

Mark 9:1-10

What does the writer of Hebrews mean by "the same" in Hebrews 13:8? Is Jesus the same in every sense or in some specific sense or senses?

How does John react to this vision of Jesus?

Why does Jesus tell John not to be afraid? What part of Jesus' words do you need to take to heart today?

According to this account, is Jesus still the image of the invisible God? Explain.

Is the incarnation permanent or temporary? Support your answer from Scripture.

How does this impact your view of your salvation?

JESUS
SWEETEST NAME I KNOW

WHO JESUS IS AND WHY IT MATTERS

An Inductive Study of Christology

OBSERVE the TEXT of SCRIPTURE

He's coming back . . . on a horse!

READ Revelation 19:11-16. **CIRCLE** every name or title give to Jesus and **UNDERLINE** every description of Him.

Revelation 19:11-16

11 *And I saw heaven opened, and behold, a white horse, and He who sat on it is called Faithful and True, and in righteousness He judges and wages war.*

12 *His eyes are a flame of fire, and on His head are many diadems; and He has a name written on Him which no one knows except Himself.*

13 *He is clothed with a robe dipped in blood, and His name is called The Word of God.*

14 *And the armies which are in heaven, clothed in fine linen, white and clean, were following Him on white horses.*

15 *From His mouth comes a sharp sword, so that with it He may strike down the nations, and He will rule them with a rod of iron; and He treads the wine press of the fierce wrath of God, the Almighty.*

16 *And on His robe and on His thigh He has a name written, "KING OF KINGS, AND LORD OF LORDS."*

DISCUSS with your GROUP or PONDER on your own . . .

Describe Jesus from the text.

How does this description compare with descriptions of Jesus prior to His ascension?

ONE STEP FURTHER:

The Names of Jesus

If you have some time this week, see how many names and/or descriptions of Jesus you can come up with from the pages of Scripture. When you list them, remember to record the reference also.

SWEETEST NAME I KNOW

WHO JESUS IS AND WHY IT MATTERS

An Inductive Study of Christology

Does this Jesus align with the Jewish hopes for a Messiah?

What titles does Jesus have in this section? What do they tell us about Him?

READ Revelation 22:12-16 where Jesus is speaking. **CIRCLE** every reference to *Jesus*, including synonyms. **UNDERLINE** everything He says He is going to do.

Revelation 22:12-16

12 *"Behold, I am coming quickly, and My reward is with Me, to render to every man according to what he has done.*

13 *"I am the Alpha and the Omega, the first and the last, the beginning and the end."*

14 *Blessed are those who wash their robes, so that they may have the right to the tree of life, and may enter by the gates into the city.*

15 *Outside are the dogs and the sorcerers and the immoral persons and the murderers and the idolaters, and everyone who loves and practices lying.*

16 *"I, Jesus, have sent My angel to testify to you these things for the churches. I am the root and the descendant of David, the bright morning star."*

DISCUSS with your GROUP or PONDER on your own . . .

What does Jesus say He is going to do when He returns?

Week Six: **Is Jesus High Priest and King?**

What two groups of people does Jesus mention?

What does Jesus call Himself in this section?

Why do these descriptions matter?

What does Jesus have to offer people?

@THE END OF THE DAY . . .

Who do you say He is? How has He changed your life?

RESOURCES

Helpful Study Tools

The New How to Study Your Bible
Eugene, Oregon: Harvest House
Publishers

The New Inductive Study Bible
Eugene, Oregon: Harvest House
Publishers

Logos Bible Software
Available at www.logos.com.

Greek Word Study Tools

Kittel, G., Friedrich, G., & Bromiley,
G.W.
*Theological Dictionary of the New
Testament, Abridged* (also known as
Little Kittel)
Grand Rapids, Michigan: W.B.
Eerdmans Publishing Company

Zodhiates, Spiros
*The Complete Word Study Dictionary:
New Testament*
Chattanooga, Tennessee: AMG
Publishers

Hebrew Word Study Tools

Harris, R.L., Archer, G.L., & Walker,
B.K.
*Theological Wordbook of the Old
Testament* (also known as TWOT)
Chicago, Illinois: Moody Press

Zodhiates, Spiros
*The Complete Word Study Dictionary:
Old Testament*
Chattanooga, Tennessee: AMG
Publishers

General Word Study Tools

Strong, James
*The New Strong's Exhaustive
Concordance of the Bible*
Nashville, Tennessee: Thomas Nelson

Recommended Commentary Sets

Expositor's Bible Commentary
Grand Rapids, Michigan: Zondervan

NIV Application Commentary
Grand Rapids, Michigan: Zondervan

The New American Commentary
Nashville, Tennessee: Broadman and
Holman Publishers

One-Volume Commentary

Carson, D.A., France, R.T., Motyer,
J.A., & Wenham, G.J. Ed.
*New Bible Commentary: 21st Century
Edition*
Downers Grove, Illinois: Inter-Varsity
Press

JESUS
SWEETEST NAME I KNOW

WHO JESUS IS AND WHY IT MATTERS

An Inductive Study of Christology

HOW TO DO AN ONLINE WORD STUDY

For use with www.blueletterbible.org

1. Type in BIble verse. Change the version to NASB. Click the "Search" button.
2. When you arrive at the next screen, you will see six lettered boxes to the left of your verse. Click the "C" button to take you to the concordance link.
3. Click on the Strong's number which is the link to the original word in Greek or Hebrew.

Clicking this number will bring up another screen that will give you a brief definition of the word as well as list every occurrence of the Greek word in the New Testament or Hebrew word in the Old Testmanet. Before running to the dictionary definition, scan places where this word is used in Scripture and examine the general contexts where it is used.

ABOUT PRECEPT

Precept Ministries International was raised up by God for the sole purpose of establishing people in God's Word to produce reverence for Him. It serves as an arm of the church without respect to denomination. God has enabled Precept to reach across denominational lines without compromising the truths of His inerrant Word. We believe every word of the Bible was inspired and given to man as all that is necessary for him to become mature and thoroughly equipped for every good work of life. This ministry does not seek to impose its doctrines on others, but rather to direct people to the Master Himself, who leads and guides by His Spirit into all truth through a systematic study of His Word. The ministry produces a variety of Bible studies and holds conferences and intensive Training Workshops designed to establish attendees in the Word through Inductive Bible Study.

Jack Arthur and his wife, Kay, founded Precept Ministries in 1970. Kay and the ministry staff of writers produce **Precept Upon Precept®** studies, **In & Out®** studies, **Lord** series studies, the **New Inductive Study Series** studies, **40-Minute** studies, and **Discover 4 Yourself Inductive Bible Studies for Kids**. From years of diligent study and teaching experience, Kay and the staff have developed these unique, inductive courses that are now used in nearly 185 countries and 70 languages.

PRECEPT NETWORK

Precept Network is an interconnected, committed group of volunteers passionately using their gifts and abilities to accomplish the mission of establishing people in God's Word!

In support of this mission, Precept Network Area Teams launched in the summer of 2012! The goal of these teams is to connect and equip Bible Study Leaders in their local communities to impact others with the life-transforming study of God's Word through the Inductive Bible Study Method. The Area Teams will provide support in states across the country. Please be in prayer for the teams as they branch out in faith to reach more and more people. If you would like to see if there is an Area Team near you, visit www.precept.org/areateams for a list of the current teams and their locations. If you do not find an Area Team close to you, you can find Bible Study Leader Enrichment Groups in our Precept Online Community. For more information, go to **www.precept.org/poc**.

ANSWERING THE CALL

Now that you've studied and prayerfully considered the scriptures, is there something new for you to believe or do, or did it move you to make a change in your life? It's one of the many amazing and supernatural results of being in His life-changing Word—God speaks to us.

At Precept Ministries International, we believe that we have heard God speak about our part in the Great Commission. He has told us in His Word to make disciples by teaching people how to study His Word. We plan to reach 10 million people with Inductive Bible Study. Note here that 2015 is removed.

If you share our passion for establishing people in God's Word, we invite you to join us! Will you prayerfully consider joining our E-Team and giving monthly to the ministry? If you give an online recurring gift as an E-Team member, fewer dollars go into administrative costs and more go toward ministry. You can join the E-Team at **www.precept.org/eteam**. You can also make a one-time gift to reach more people with Inductive Bible Study at **www.precept.org/ATC**. Please pray about how the Lord might lead you to answer the call.

PURCHASE WITH PURPOSE

When you buy books, studies, videos and audios, please purchase from Precept Ministries through our online store **(http://store.precept.org/)**. We realize you may find some of these materials at a lower price through for-profit retailers, but when you buy through us, the proceeds support the work that we do to:

- Develop new Inductive Bible studies
- Translate more studies into other languages
- Support efforts in nearly 185 countries
- Reach millions daily through radio and television
- Train pastors and Bible Study Leaders around the world
- Develop inductive studies for children to start their journey with God
- Equip people of all ages with Bible Study skills that transform lives

When you buy from Precept, you help to **establish people in God's Word!**

WHO JESUS IS AND WHY IT MATTERS

An Inductive Study of Christology

PAM GILLASPIE

Pam Gillaspie, a passionate Bible student and teacher, authors Precept's *Sweeter Than Chocolate!*® and *Cookies on the Lower Shelf*™ Bible study series. Pam holds a BA in Biblical Studies from Wheaton College in Wheaton, Illinois. She and her husband live in suburban Chicago, Illinois with their son, daughter, and Great Dane. Her greatest joy is encouraging others to read God's Word widely and study it deeply . . . precept upon precept.

Connect with Pam at:

www.deepandwide.org

 pamgillaspie

 pamgillaspie

CPSIA information can be obtained at www.ICGtesting.com
Printed in the USA
LVOW02s2019160913

352741LV00003B/6/P